Praying a Blessing for Someone

Why waste your time worrying for a loved one, when you could spend that same time praying powerful prayers of salvation, breakthrough, and blessings instead? Join Eric Sprinkle and Laura Shaffer as they give you the blueprint for prayers that make a world of difference.

> Linda Evans Shepherd, bestselling author of
> *Praying God's Promises* and *Praying Through Every Emotion*

Praying for Someone's Salvation

Thoroughly comprehensive, practical, clear, inspiring and helpful. HIGHLY recommend.
Laura Shaffer along with Eric Sprinkle, has used her gentle, comprehensive and long-ranging experience of intercessory prayer to compose a guiding book which is user-friendly, encouraging and hope-inspiring. Hang on in there. Keep praying.

> | Early Amazon Reviewer

I like this book because the prayers are sooo much more powerful and give me ideas on what words to use through the day. See, I'm 8 1/2 and my friends at school do not know Jesus. This helps me focus.

> | Amazon Reviewer (with Mom)

I've been doing the *40 Day Prayer Guides—Praying for Someone's Salvation* for about 2 weeks now and it's such a huge blessing. The prayers are wonderful, and working through each day's prayers has definitely been a blessing to me each morning. I am actively seeking time with the person I am praying for as a result of praying for him and we have had a lot of fun... plus it has laid a groundwork of trust for God to work in through our conversations.

> | Robin Shear, professional Joy Coach, author of the JOY BITES blog & an upcoming book about finding joy despite difficult circumstances. (www.joytotheworldcoaching.com)

Praise for the 40 Day Prayer Guide series

You two make such a great team. Not only is Laura's content rich and practical, but Eric's photos also add a powerful and needed dimension to the prayers. Well done!

> Dick Bruso, Branding/Marketing Expert and Founder of "Heard Above The Noise"

I love the images and photos in these books. They are such an inspiration! Some of them excite me, others spark my imagination. And sometimes, one of them will completely transport me away to another place. A beautiful, quiet place, far away from life's stresses, where I can sit for a minute, reflecting on God's goodness, and on my wonderful prayer time with Him.

> Susan Neal, RN, MBA, MHA Director, Christian Indie Publishers Association, and best-selling author of *7 Steps to Get Off Sugar and Carbohydrates*

You can pick up this book and begin praying immediately because the prayers are right there for you. Laura guides us as a "prayer warrior," sharing her words and letting us make them our own. Thanks to this book, applying prayer is easier than ever before."

> Laine Lawson Craft, best-selling author of *Enjoy Today Own Tomorrow*

As a mental health therapist, I'm always looking for ways to help my clients from a holistic perspective and this book is a great resource to do just that! The combination of breathtaking photos and spirit-sparking prayers is a great asset to anyone looking to enhance their journey through the power of prayer.

> Gina Birkemeier, LPC and award-winning author of *Generations Deep: Unmasking Inherited Dysfunction and Trauma to Rewrite Our Stories Through Faith and Therapy*

40 DAY PRAYER GUIDES

Praying for Godly Character

Powerful day-by-day prayers inviting God to Strengthen your Character

Eric Sprinkle and Laura Shaffer

Praying for Godly Character: Powerful day-by-day prayers inviting God to Strengthen your Character

Copyright @ 2022 Eric Sprinkle and Laura Shaffer

All rights reserved. No part of this publication may be reproduced or transmitted in any form or by any electronic or mechanical means including photo copying, recording, or any information storage and retrieval system now known or to be invented, without permission in writing from the publisher or the author.

Scriptures taken from the Holy Bible, New International Version®, NIV®. Copyright © 1973, 1978, 1984, 2011 by Biblica, Inc.™ Used by permission of Zondervan. All rights reserved worldwide. www.zondervan.com The "NIV" and "New International Version" are trademarks registered in the United States Patent and Trademark Office by Biblica, Inc.™

All photos by Eric Sprinkle
Cover and interior design by Robin Black

ISBN: 978-1-7322694-4-6

Published by Adventure Experience Press in partnership with the fine folks at EA Books Books Publishing, a division of
Living Parables of Central Florida, Inc. a 501c3

AdventureExperience.net
EABooksPublishing.com

DEDICATIONS

Laura
To my parents and grandparents and those who
came before me who knew God and turned to Him in good
times and bad: Tom and Truda Fail, HC and Odessa Fail, DW
and my Minnie Gray, characters one and all. They taught me
to love God, love my country, and love my family.
I stand, not alone, but on their shoulders.

Eric
To the 2004 "Add-a-Loon" Club. The very first rafters on the Arkansas River each year, simply by daring to go whitewater rafting every Jan 1st. In Colorado. Chilly temps, dragging boats across ice bridges, and running narrow icy chutes through frozen Class IV rapids. They exemplified what Daring, Courage, and reasonable Risk-Taking all looked like, and for some reason invited me along too, cementing my love of crazy adventures to this very day.

ACKNOWLEDGEMENTS

- To Robin, Rebecca, and the Team at EA Books that helped us once again take this book from concept, to reality.
- Eric also thanks Team Editor Amy, for taking time out of the Carolina springtime for a quick look at our work.
- Laura—I owe a debt of gratitude to my amazing prayer partners over the years who have been a blessing in my life, teaching me how to pray by example through our Torah group, Moms in Prayer groups, Community groups, and Bible studies.
- Extra special thanks go to Cathy, my 40 Day partner who prayed with me through the 40 Day prayers, and our Revive Small Group. Their prayers and encouragement were invaluable.
- Lastly and always, to our Gracious Lord God, who not only hears our prayers and has blessed us with His character traits, but continues to bless us as we seek to use them for His glory, far beyond what we could ever dare to ask or imagine. *Soli Deo Gloria* indeed.

INTRODUCTION TO 40 DAYS

Let's face it, our gracious Lord God has a thing for 40 days. Forty days of rain to flood the earth, 40 days spent in the wilderness before Jesus started his ministry, 40 days before the clock ran down on Nineveh to return to Him. Over and over, we see 40 days as the time frame God uses for major changes in people and circumstances.

God also loves it when we talk to and share with Him through prayer. Share our thoughts, our fears, our celebrations, and concerns. The Bible tells us it's our prayers and petitions, with thanksgiving, that God uses to bring us peace (Phil 4:6-7). Jesus himself told the disciples that sometimes when casting out demons only prayer will do the trick (Mark 9:29).

So what about you? How do you feel about committing 40 days towards a goal? Could the book you're holding be your opportunity to ask God to bless you in a way you've never thought of before? Praying for Him to plant seeds for new character traits in your heart and mind. Maybe even awaken ones you never even suspected were there?

Okay, let's change things up then. Let's make beautiful, Bible-based, laser-focused prayers a part of our daily routine for the next 40 days. Prayers for just you. Prayers for your character, the root of how you think, act and feel towards the world around us. And instead of trying to think of the words, instead we'll simply use some of the wonderful, powerful, stirring prayers from our mutual friend, Laura.

Let's read her prayers and make them our own. Let's pray them silently or aloud, inserting and praying your own personal thoughts and reflections along the way. Don't worry, it'll all be automatic by the time you get to Day 4.

What if we add a second person to pray for? Maybe your spouse? What if we invite someone else to pray with us too? Inviting a grandparent to join you on this 40 day prayer journey in praying this book over you, and one of your kiddos or friends? All lifting up these prayers for life giving, God honoring character to appear and be made known in our lives. To us, and to those around us. That the hurting in the world would be helped, the weak offered a hand, and that those needing a kind word would each find it through us. To God's glory alone, forever and always.

I say we find out.

It's time to turn the page and begin a 40 day journey, focused on praying for God to open the floodgates of Heaven, bestowing a little, or a lot, of the gifts, skills, abilities, and character traits we've all seen and read about, over-and-over again, throughout the Bible.

Are you ready?

Let's do this.

Introduction to Character

How do you live your life? How do you make choices when facing decisions? What guides you.?
   Your character.
What you feel down deep inside springs from what you believe. About yourself. About the world. About God. About whether you believe there is some sort of reckoning or judgement when your life on earth is done. And it forms the qualities/attributes that make up your character.

Most of us want to believe that we are good. But our definition of what is good varies. It may depend on the changing values of the times we live in. Or the culture we were raised in. And our ability to behave as we want to can be affected by lots of factors: hunger, anger, loneliness, frustration, fatigue.

The Bible has a lot to say about character and the values that God regards as good. We can read about them in the people we meet in scripture.

Of course, Jesus is the perfect example. He came to be a walking, breathing example for godly living. Yet most of us believe we can't live up to Jesus' perfect example. For years a popular cultural phrase had people asking "What Would Jesus Do?" whenever a circumstance arose that posed a question of the right way to behave. The answer was to look in the Bible and see how Jesus lived his life. Then apply those characteristics of his behavior to our situation, choosing to behave in that way and live a better, more godly life.

Many times we might naturally behave in a godly way. But sometimes our first inclination may be to go the other direction. Or we may behave out of selfishness, greed, stress, or immaturity.

The good news is we can change. We can invite God to build our character biblically. When we recognize what direction we want to go we can embrace a new value that will change our behavior, and over time develop a new trait as part of our character.

As always, the purpose of our books is to encourage you and give you some tools to be more intentional and consistent in prayer. And in spending time in prayer, deepen your relationship with God, and hear what He wants to say to you.

Change takes time. And we will make mistakes. But character develops from our beliefs and repeated behavior. So if we change our behaviors based on what we believe, that becomes our new character.

The 40 Day Prayer Guide: Praying for Godly Character is here to help you observe some ordinary people who displayed extraordinary character, and observe their behavior. When you find a specific quality that you would benefit from embracing, the prayers will guide you in asking God to strengthen your own character..

The Characters

These are people like us—not perfect. They have made mistakes, some of them serious and costly. We can see ourselves in them, and learn from them.

The Characteristics

Not an exhaustive list of every quality a godly person should possess. But some good places to start.

How to Use this 40 Day Prayer Guide

Prayer pages:

The guide will give you one character trait to pray for each day for 40 days.

You can simply pray the prayer as it is, or you can let the Holy Spirit guide you and use your own words.

Or these prayers can be a springboard for your prayer time as the Holy Spirit brings more things to mind as you pray.

For instance, there may be times when a particular problem or situation will take precedence over a pre-planned agenda of prayer.

And there may be times when the Holy Spirit leads you to a different topic. Go for it!

Being flexible and sensitive to the Holy Spirit is the most important thing. Simply being intentional and consistent in your prayer time will help you be sensitive to the Holy Spirit.

Reflection Pages:

Every 7 days the Guide will give you opportunities to:
- Write down your thoughts as you go along.
- Evaluate your progress.
- Look for ways God may be answering your prayers and thank Him.
- See how He is speaking to you personally about your prayer life, or how God might be leading you in your life.

There are, of course, many things you can pray to strengthen your character. This is not meant to list or speak to all of them.

It will, however, help you be more intentional and consistent in praying. And by spending time in prayer, you will be open to the Spirit's leading. Learning to listen to the Holy Spirit guide you is most important.

It is our desire to help you grow in your prayer life as you pray. That you will benefit from the answers to your prayers. And that you will be blessed as you *Lean in and Learn from the Lord* through prayer.

Before Beginning

Reflections page...Are you willing to set aside a few minutes each day to pray?

We hope to encourage you and accompany you on your 40 day journey with day by day prayers. We also understand that sometimes things get in the way that are unavoidable. If you have to miss a day, simply pick up where you left off. You don't want to miss out on a blessing or on hearing from God.

It may help to find a specific place or regular time of day to be sure you are being intentional and consistent in your praying. (like when you first get up, or while exercising, on your way to work or during a break from work, or in a room or seat in your home at a certain time, or at a natural break in your daily routine).

When praying, there is wisdom in preparing yourself. Two areas are important:

1. **Confession and Repentance**—The Bible tells us in Psalm 66:18, "If I had cherished sin in my heart, the Lord would not have listened." So it is important to take time to ask God to search your heart and show you any sin you need to confess and repent of before you move into interceding for someone.

    God has promised that "If we confess our sins, He is faithful and just and will forgive us our sins and purify us from all unrighteousness." 1 John 1:9.

2. **Spiritual Armor for Battle**—Ephesians tells us to be "Strong in the Lord and in His mighty power. Put on the full armor of God." 6:10-11. So we need to do that—name and pray on each piece before we pray for others.

Page 102 in the Appendix at the back of this book will walk you through these steps.

Prayer tips

Are all prayers equal? It seems that God has listed some guidelines for us in Scripture that can either compromise or boost the effectiveness of our prayers.

There are even things that can cause Him to choose to step back or even disregard our prayers for a time. Yikes! Others are just the opposite, creating a multiplying effect on our prayers.

Have a look through and make sure nothing listed is going to get in your way over the next 40 days.

Some Biblical Guidelines

"The prayer of a righteous person is powerful and effective" (James 5:16).

Be sure you're following God and steering away from anything unrighteous or purposefully against God's ways for living. Holding grudges, being angry, indulging in wrongful thoughts or actions can all take away from the effectiveness of your 40 day journey.

"The eyes of the Lord are on the righteous, and his ears are attentive to their cry" (Psalm 34:15).

Exactly the opposite, we can rest assured we have God's complete attention when pursuing right living in our actions and choices.

"Then Jesus told his disciples a parable to show them that they should always pray and not give up" (Luke 18:1).

No worries there, you're going to be praying for the next 40 days, so you've got this!

"When you ask you do not receive, because you ask with wrong motives, that you may spend what you get on your pleasures" (James 4:3).

Okay, so praying for Wisdom and Daring just so you can get a promotion at work is sketchy. Doing it all for that same raise and then buying new shoes is right out.

"But your iniquities have separated you from your God; your sins have hidden his face from you, so that he will not hear" (Isaiah 59:2).

Again, let's be careful we don't have sin in our hearts that will get in the way of what we're asking. If we want to see the stars, let's get away from light pollution. If we want to talk to God, let's clear out the background noise and use a strong signal with four bars.

"This is the confidence we have in approaching God: that if we ask anything according to his will, he hears us" (1 John 5:14).

Let's all be sure we're asking for things in line with His will, His plans, His timing, and not our own. Trust that God is actively working to draw this person to Him, and bless them for His Glory, even if we're not seeing anything happening right away.

Additional ideas that can boost the impact of your praying

Pray these prayers out loud.
Does it help God hear them better? No. Does it help you? You bet! Praying out loud helps you slow down and focus on the person and words you're praying - allowing time for the Holy Spirit to meet you in your prayer. And that can make a difference all on its own.

As the Holy Spirit brings additional things to mind when you're praying, pray those too.
The Holy Spirit knows best what you are getting at in your prayers to the Father.

Pray the daily prayer multiple times a day.
When you eat? Morning and Evening? Or maybe whenever you start your car?

Pray for more than one person.
What happens if you pray each prayer for you, and a kiddo? Or someone else God brings to mind that day?

Pray this 40 Day journey along with a friend.
Both of you, praying for your own Character, but checking in with each other on your journeys.

Consider fasting at some point during the journey.
Giving up TV, social media, or even certain foods for a week during your journey will only serve to sharpen your spiritual focus!

Don't miss the Appendix Resources

Check out our Appendix at the back of this book for valuable resources you might need during your 40 Day Journey. Whether that's how to better hear and discern God's voice, "armoring up" against spiritual push-back, or explaining a prayerful discipline like "fasting" in step-by-step language. We've got you covered..

Table of Contents

Day 1	My Commitment	1
Day 2	*Obedient*—Noah	3
Day 3	*Hineni*—Abraham	5
Day 4	*Adventurous*—Rebekah	7
Day 5	*Resilient*—Jacob	9
Day 6	*Forgiving*—Joseph	11
Day 7	*Teachable*—Moses	13
Day 8	*Creative*—Bezalel and Oholiab	17
Day 9	*Courageous*—Joshua and Caleb	19
Day 10	*Bold*—Rahab	21
Day 11	*Humble*—Ruth	23
Day 12	*Earnest*—Hannah	25
Day 13	*Honorable*—Samuel	27
Day 14	*Confident*—David	29
Day 15	*Ready to act*—David's Fighting Men	33
Day 16	*Discerning*—Men of Issachar	37
Day 17	*Diplomatic*—Abigail	39
Day 18	*Wise*—Solomon	41
Day 19	*Trusting God*—Jehoshaphat	43
Day 20	*Powerful Pray-er*—Hezekiah	45
Day 21	*Responsive*—Josiah	47
Day 22	*Dedicated*—Daniel	53
Day 23	*Authentic*—Ezra	55
Day 24	*Self-Controlled*—Nehemiah	57
Day 25	*Risk-Taker*—Esther	59
Day 26	*God-fearing*—Job	61
Day 27	*Hopeful*—Habakkuk	63
Day 28	*Joyful*—Mary	65
Day 29	*Passionate*—Woman at the Well	69
Day 30	*Simple Faith*—The Royal Official	71
Day 31	*Generous*—Poor Widow	73

Day 32 *Committed*—Paralyzed man's friends. 75
Day 33 *Curious*—Zacchaeus. 77
Day 34 *Daring*—Bleeding Woman 79
Day 35 *Caring*—Good Samaritan 81
Day 36 *Thankful*—The One Leper. 85
Day 37 *Persistent*—The Blind Beggar. 87
Day 38 *Encourager*—Paul. 89
Day 39 You choose 91
Day 40 Aaronic Blessing. 93
Priestly Blessing 95
Thank You Prayer 99

Appendix A Confession and Repentance 101
Appendix B Spiritual Armor for Battle 102
Appendix C How you tune in to God's voice 105
Appendix D Tune In Exercise for Hearing God 107
Appendix E Hearing from God. 109
Appendix F Hearing from God Worksheet 111
Appendix G Fasting 112
About the Authors 115

Oh Lord Strengthen Me

I feel You here I hear Your voice
and yet I find no reason to rejoice
For You have called me to Your side
and as unworthy as I am I want to hide

You give me choices You make me free Oh Lord strengthen me

In other times I knew Your will
and I became the vessel You could fill
Why is it hard now to take a stand
when I have seen the power in Your hand

You give me choices You make me free Oh Lord strengthen me

Lead me hold me
guide me Lord enfold me
cover me with the blood of Calvary
and be with me
be with me

Oh let me make Your strength my own
and let me feel it flowing from Your precious throne
right by Your side oh let me be
and let me feel Your power washing over me
You give me choices
You make me free oh Lord
strengthen me
Oh Lord, Oh Lord strengthen me
                1994 Laura Shaffer

DAY 1

My Commitment

Ephesians 3:14, 16-17, *For this reason I kneel before the Father... I pray that out of his glorious riches he may strengthen you with power through his Spirit in your inner being, so that Christ may dwell in your hearts through faith.*

Heavenly Father, I am offering these prayers in the power of the name of the Lord Jesus Christ. I am trusting You to act and effect Your will during these next 40 days of prayer for my character.

I want to be more like Christ in my attitudes and my actions. As a Christian, I desire to display the character of a mature believer. When You walked on this earth Luke tells me that You grew in wisdom, and stature, and in favor with God and man (Luke 2:52). So I am praying for these 40 days that You will show me how to develop godly character, putting off those characteristics I may have that do not honor You, and putting on those that will.

I know that the devil and the world and even my own flesh can be enemies of this process. Help me recognize these when they are at work against me. And be at work in my life in ways that help me overcome any evil forces at work here.

Spread Your protection over my body, mind and spirit. Watch over my physical health so no accident or illness sidelines me. Meet my emotional needs where relationships have broken down. Heal any spiritual wounds where I have been hurt by other Christians or by believing lies.

Father, work in my life in ways that only You can, especially during these 40 days of prayer.

As for me, I will set aside time each of these 40 days and be open to hear from You, from scripture, and in prayer. And will look into these biblical characters to see how they will speak to me about changes I need to make, or attitudes I need to embrace, or encouragement I need to hear.

Father, help me in my commitment to pray daily. I give this 40-day journey to You. Lead me and teach me as I seek Your wisdom and direction for developing godly character. I humbly ask for Your will to be done in and through my life.

Open up Your storehouse of blessing and encouragement, and strengthen me with godly character. Amen

Noah found favor in Your eyes. He was a righteous man who walked faithfully with You in the midst of a culture that did not follow You. He heard Your voice clearly, even to the specific details of how to build an ark. And he responded with complete obedience despite his advanced age, the time it took to accomplish the task, and the amount of work that was required.

DAY 2

Noah—Obedient

Genesis 6:9, *Noah was a righteous man, blameless among the people of his time, and he walked faithfully with God.*

Heavenly Father, show me how to live a righteous life, to draw away from the violent, corrupt, evil influences in my society today in obedience to Your call. Whether in my business or personal life, when I am tempted: by my own appetites, by the attraction of what the world offers, or by the evil one, give me the strength to overcome temptation and take the way of escape You provide. Help me live by Your values, not the values of the world or whatever my culture calls correct at the moment.

Let me remember that I am Your child and find strength in that relationship, not bowing to social or political pressures. Remind me to schedule quiet time with You, reading the Bible, walking in nature, or worshipping You through music and prayer. Speak to me of values, attitudes, behaviors I may need to change to live a life of obedience. When You speak to me let me hear You as Noah did: in a way that I recognize and understand.

Father, help me respond in complete obedience, doing all that You command. Whether I am young or old. Whether I can accomplish it quickly or it takes a long time. Whether it's easy or takes all I have to give. Give me the perseverance and strength to do what You call me to. Empower me to withstand any opposition to complete all that You ask, living a purpose driven life.

Father, strengthen my character to be like Noah: Obedient, in how I live amid an ungodly culture, and obedient to the purposes You reveal to me. Amen

Read more about Noah: Genesis 6:5-7:24

Abram, who God renamed Abraham,
answered God's call by saying "Hineni"
or "Here am I." Much more than just
an indication of bring present, this is a deep
surrender of service and self to be obedient
to a call. Abraham left his home and
set off in the direction God gave without
a specific destination, but with a great
promise, fulfilled generations later
in his descendant, Jesus Christ.

DAY 3

Abraham—Hineni—Here am I

Genesis 22:9, *God tested Abraham. He said to him, "Abraham!" "Here I am," he replied*

Heavenly Father, show me how to listen for Your voice and respond to what You say to me with a sense of awe and respect like Abraham.

Help me be willing to leave behind whatever is necessary to follow You wherever You say to go—even if I don't understand at the time. Even if what You ask is difficult. Even if it takes more time and I don't see results right away.

As I come to You in prayer, I will make time to not only speak, but also listen. I will seek Your counsel in decisions I make in my personal life, my relationships, in my business and financial dealings. Open my ears to the message of Your words that bring personal meaning and conviction to my life.

Let me be ready, not to just be present for what You want, but count it as an honor and privilege to take responsibility, even change my course if necessary to fully obey; trusting You completely with the outcome.

And let this be a pattern for my life as it was with Abraham. Not just a one-time special circumstance of obedience because it's convenient. Let my life resound with Hineni! And let me mean what I say: that I hear Your voice, I understand what You are asking. And I am ready and willing to do it!

Father, strengthen my character to be like Abraham: able to respond to You, Hineni! Amen.

Read more about Abraham: Genesis 12, 15, 17, 22

When given a choice to go or stay, Rebekah chose
to go immediately and become the wife of Isaac,
Abraham's son, giving up all she knew: the familiarity
of family and friends and a place and style of living.
She set out with a stranger, whom You had blessed and led
to her. And later, when confused by her pregnancy,
she sought You and received a revelation.

DAY 4

Rebekah—Adventurous

Genesis 24:58, *So they called Rebekah and asked her, "Will you go with this man?"*
"I will go," she said.

Heavenly Father, let me be adventurous like Rebekah; willing to go when You say "Go." Let my faith and trust in You be so strong, it overpowers all other concerns, worries, or obstacles. Even when it shows up unexpectedly and takes me in a completely new direction or far away from home. Help me be willing to accept changes in my environment, or circle of friends, or circumstances to be in the place where You lead me.

Reveal to me, as You did to Rebekah, when something is *"from the Lord."* When I see how You have prepared a way, do not let me delay; but go quickly in obedience with courage, anticipating all You have for me. I trust that regardless of how the world looks, if I am in the center of Your will, it is the safest place for me.

And when I am confused by life's circumstances, let me not be fearful, or seek the wisdom of the world. But draw close to You and seek Your perspective and explanation. So I'm not leaning on my own understanding, give me a fresh perspective of my difficulties. Send a revelation that directs my adventurous path and encourages me in the way I should go.

Like Rebekah, I want to place all my security in You. Even when the world can offer no sense of safety. When circumstances seem radically out of control and way beyond my comfort level, help me choose to trust You.

Father, strengthen my character to be like Rebekah: Adventurous, in response to You. Amen

Read more about Rebekah: Genesis 24:12-61; 25:19-26

Jacob, renamed Israel by God, was Rebekah's son, a twin. Forced to leave home after a deception to gain his birthright, he was in turn deceived by his father-in-law over his wife, then his flocks. But God's promise was passed down from Abraham to Isaac, to Jacob. He had twelve sons who became the twelve tribes of Israel. One of his sons, his beloved Joseph was believed dead, but was found safe and prosperous in Egypt and saved all his family from the famine so they could eventually enter God's Promised Land.

DAY 5

Jacob—Resilient

Genesis 32:24-26; 28, *So Jacob was left alone, and a man wrestled with him till daybreak. When the man saw that he could not overpower him, he touched the socket of Jacob's hip so that his hip was wrenched as he wrestled with the man. Then the man said, "Let me go, for it is daybreak."*
But Jacob replied, "I will not let you go unless you bless me."
Then the man said, "Your name will no longer be Jacob, but Israel, because you have struggled with God and with humans and have overcome."

Heavenly Father, make me resilient, able to handle the ups and downs of life like Jacob. His childhood had its ups and downs. Then after leaving home he was deceived in matters of love, marriage, business. In my life there have been ups and downs too: times of delirious joy as well as tragic disappointment and sorrow. Sometimes I feel I can barely get up for another day. Strengthen me to be able to handle downturns and adverse circumstances. To be able to learn from them and tolerate the time it takes to recover.

Jacob lost a wife, a son, had parenting and family issues, reversals at work, and natural disasters, much like people face today. Yet, even in times like this, You call on people to be resilient, obedient, to take a stand or make a move. Father, in those times, prune away any misunderstanding and revive me to be fruitful again.

When my life has fallen apart with tragedy and stress, thank You for sending the Holy Spirit to comfort me. Thank You for bringing friends around for the support I need. Thank You for Your Word, the Bible, with encouraging scriptures. And praise music. Thank You for all these ways I can deal with grief and the stress of life's ups and downs. Revive me! Tune my ears to Your call, and help me bounce back, and continue to trust in You.

Father, strengthen my character to be like Jacob: Resilient through the ups and downs of life. Amen

Read more about Jacob: Genesis 25:19-34; 27-35

Joseph was Jacob's beloved and favored son.
God was with Joseph in every hard circumstance of his life,
mistreated by brothers, sold into slavery by them,
wrongly accused and imprisoned. After years of hardship,
God placed him in a position in Egypt to save his entire
family from famine. With their confession,
he forgave all the evil done to him, crediting God
with his deliverance and their salvation.

DAY 6

Joseph—Forgiving

Genesis 50:18-20, *His brothers then came and threw themselves down before him. "We are your slaves," they said.*
But Joseph said to them, "Don't be afraid. Am I in the place of God? You intended to harm me, but God intended it for good to accomplish what is now being done, the saving of many lives.

Heavenly Father, if anyone had a right to be bitter and vindictive, it was Joseph. There are things in my life too, times I was taken advantage of, cheated, treated unfairly. And to be honest, if I had the ability to inflict some sort of judgement or revenge it would be hard to pass it up. Forgive me for being so self-centered that I would think only of my own interests and feelings.

Although evil is in this world and even in positions of power and authority, it is nothing compared to You and Your ability to preserve Your will. Despite slavery, prison and the murderous jealousy and greed of Joseph's brothers, You were able to use it all to accomplish the deliverance of Your people from the years of famine and more. And the hardships in my life have not been so great as that.

It has been said that unforgiveness is like drinking poison and expecting the other person to die. Don't let unforgiveness make me sick, bitter and unhappy. Don't allow past events to keep me chained to the offense. Put my focus on You, seeking Your perspective and Your presence. That can do more for me than going down the road of revenge.

Vengeance belongs to You. Father, remind me to seek You when I face hardships and challenges and downright evil. Let me walk in the freedom of forgiveness.

Father, strengthen my character to be like Joseph: Forgiving, even after enduring so much. Amen

Read more about Joseph: Genesis 37, 39, 41-50

Moses was a Hebrew born in Egypt at a time when the Pharaoh had ordered the death of all male Hebrew babies. God miraculously delivered Moses to be raised in the Pharaoh's palace. After learning of his true heritage and killing an Egyptian, he fled to the wilderness where after forty years God spoke to him in a burning bush, charging Moses to lead the Hebrews out of Egyptian slavery and into the Promised land to fulfill His promise to Abraham, Isaac and Jacob.

DAY 7

Moses—Teachable

Exodus 4:10-12, *Moses said to the Lord, "Pardon your servant, Lord. I have never been eloquent, neither in the past nor since you have spoken to your servant. I am slow of speech and tongue."*

The Lord said to him, "Who gave human beings their mouths? Who makes them deaf or mute? Who gives them sight or makes them blind? Is it not I, the Lord? Now go; I will help you speak and will teach you what to say."

Heavenly Father, Moses' life was full of change. In our lives, we may deal with living in different places, going to different schools, having different jobs, meeting different people and being aware of different cultures. Even living in the same place can offer changing times.

Thank You that you are with me in every change I go through, as You were with Moses. Thank You that You help me learn how to live in all these differing geographical, cultural and social environments and in the midst of it all, teach me how to live a godly life.

You have promised to "teach me in the way I should go." (Psalm 32:8) Help me be sensitive to the ways You communicate with me. Perhaps not a burning bush, but from Your Word, in prayer, through nature, blessing, pain, other people, circumstances. Let me hear all You have to teach me about You; how to seek You, communicate with You, worship You, and serve You. And how You work in my life to prepare me for the work You have for me to do.

Help me be open to learn new things, and unlearn things I thought I knew but are not right or of value to You. Let me see clearly how You direct my path, as You teach me how to interact with those around me. When I make mistakes, I am reassured that You don't waste anything and are able to help me learn from the mistakes I make.

Whether in relationships, finances, career, health, family, travel, ministry, social or political issues, rather than lean on my own understanding, I choose to remain open and teachable in the ways I make decisions and react to hardship and challenges.

Father, strengthen my character to be like Moses: Teachable. Amen

Read more about Moses: Genesis

Reflections

How are you doing so far? If you have been able to be consistent in praying this week – good for you!
> If not, what has gotten in your way and how can you remedy that?

_____
_____

> If you got off track, just pick up where you left off.

During your prayer time this week, what has God shown you about Himself?

_____
_____

> About yourself?

_____
_____

In thinking back over the prayers this week...
> Which of the characteristics would you say already describe you? Think of an example of when you demonstrated that trait.

_____
_____

> Did any of the characters or characteristics stand out to you? Why?

Noah, Abraham and Moses all heard God's voice and responded with obedience. What do you think you're hearing God say to you?

_____

If it helps, use the sheet in the Appendix to confirm what you're hearing.
If you aren't hearing from God, ask Him to speak to you today.

Check out the Appendix for some ways you might tune in to God's voice in your life.

> If you are hearing, but not obeying, ask God to show you why not. And to give you the courage to move forward into His will and over or around any obstacles. Write how He responds to you and any steps you should take.

_____

_____

Jacob and Joseph both had tremendous ups and downs in their lives. Yet they were able to cope with them and not grow bitter, even forgiving those who mistreated them. Looking back now, list some down times and how God has worked through them.

_____

_____

> If you're in a down time now, ask God to keep you strong. Ask for a sense of His presence to keep you going through what you're experiencing.

_____

_____

Vengeance belongs to God. Joseph said "Am I in the place of God?" as he forgave his brothers. Are there people or things you need to forgive? Write their names here. Ask God to show you how to avoid bitterness and what steps to take to move forward into forgiveness.

_____

_____

Are there things in your life that are confusing? Or opportunities you are unsure about? Like Rebekah, ask God to show you if and how He is moving in your life so you can respond with going forward or understanding the circumstances.

_____

_____

When the Lord commanded Moses to build a Tabernacle, He chose Bezalel and Oholiab and filled them with the wisdom, knowledge and skills needed to accomplish the work. They were artists, metallurgists, stonecutters, perfumers, and could work with wood, engraving, embroiders, and were given the ability to teach others. Both rose to the occasion using their gifts, effectively with others.

DAY 8

Bezalel and Oholiab—Creative

Exodus 35:30-31, 34, *See, the Lord has chosen Bezalel... and he has filled him with the Spirit of God, with wisdom, with understanding, with knowledge and with all kinds of skills... And he has given both him and Oholiab... the ability to teach others.*

Heavenly Father, You are a creative God - You created the entire universe and everything in it! Every sun, moon, star and planet, every plant, animal, and human being represent Your infinite power of diversity and creativity. And You created me in Your image. So, although not to the extent You are, I am creative too.

Show me the unique way You have created me; the personality, passions, abilities, experiences and spiritual gifts You have blessed me with. If I am not aware of these pieces that make up who I am, lead me to make time to discover them. You have a purpose for the way You made me, and I believe the more I am able to use these gifts and talents the more fulfilled I will be.

In giving every believer spiritual gifts, help me accept who I am and what I have to offer. Sometimes I shrink back thinking my gift isn't as valuable as someone else's. Take away the doubts I have when it comes to my gifts. Help me refine the creativity and the spiritual gifts You've given me, and develop them to be ready to be used when the opportunity comes.

Open my eyes to every opportunity You give me to use these gifts and abilities, whether in work, ministry, my community or family. Help me see Your plan and Your purpose and be bold in doing my part.

Father, strengthen my character to be like Bezalel and Oholiab: Creative; aware of my creativity and gifts and ready and willing to use them. Amen

Read more about Bezalel and Oholiab: Exodus: 35:30 - 39:43

Joshua and Caleb were among the twelve who explored the Promised land when the Israelites came from Egypt. They were the only two who were not afraid of the people who lived there and stood fearless, trusting God would deliver this good land into their hands.

DAY 9

Joshua and Caleb—Courageous

Numbers 14:6-9, *Joshua and Caleb, who were among those who had explored the land, tore their clothes and said to the entire Israelite assembly, "The land we passed through and explored is exceedingly good. If the Lord is pleased with us, he will lead us into that land, a land flowing with milk and honey, and will give it to us. Only do not rebel against the Lord. And do not be afraid of the people of the land.*

Heavenly Father, make me courageous like Joshua and Caleb. Do not let me compare the size of the enemy to my own strength and be filled with fear and dread. Or spread that fear and rebellion to others. But like Joshua and Caleb, remind me to compare the enemy to the size and strength of my Great God who has promised me an abundant life—You!

When I look at my circumstances, remind me that I am not alone...that I can call on You—my Ally:
> The One who can do miracles!
> The One who keeps His promises!
> The One who is faithful to His Word!

I do not want to listen to the voices of the world or the enemy who wants to keep me fearful, discouraged and overwhelmed. Do not let fear get the better of me but help me seek out Your promises and hold to those even in the face of trials and trouble.

Let me see that the future You have promised me is exceedingly good. Forgive me when I have given up before the battle has even begun. Forgive me when I have focused on the challenges before me instead of the Ally standing beside me.

Help me realize that when You are with me, there is no protection for the enemy. Lead me into my promised land and help me take possession of it.

Father, strengthen my character to be like Joshua and Caleb: Courageous because of my faith in You. Amen

Read more about Joshua and Caleb: Numbers 13:1 - 14:38

Rahab, although a prostitute in the pagan city of Jericho, was courageous enough to defy her king and protect two Israelite men who came to spy out the land for Joshua. Having heard of all God had done for the Israelites, she had a fear and respect of the Lord, and acted on it. Rahab saved her family and was part of the bloodline of Jesus.

DAY 10

Rahab—Bold

Joshua 6:17, *Only Rahab the prostitute and all who are with her in her house shall be spared, because she hid the spies we sent.*

Heavenly Father, there are many authorities and powers in my life. Some are trustworthy, but some are driven by ungodly motives from the lure of the world and the lust of the flesh. They would lead me away from a God-fearing lifestyle. Help me recognize when I should obey my authorities, and when I need to have the boldness to stand up for what is right in Your eyes. Give me the grit and boldness that Rahab had when I need to make hard decisions and go against wrongful authority in my life.

Father I am in awe of You and Your amazing power. You are sovereign over all earthly authorities. If there is a conflict between what someone else is telling me to do, and what You are, speak to me so I understand how and when to act. In making decisions where there are choices, do not let me be tempted to just choose the easy way. When there is a right way or a direction You want me to go, lead me. Sometimes it's hard to do the right thing and fear takes hold. If necessary, help me do the right thing even if I am afraid.

I am Your child and trust You will protect me when I respond to what You call me to do. In those circumstances, make me bold in taking action. Even in the face of potential trouble coming back on me, strengthen me. Help me remember that being in the center of Your will is the safest place I can be. Show me how to use what I have to facilitate Your plan and bring You honor.

Father, strengthen my character to be like Rahab: Bold. Amen

Read more about Rahab: Joshua 2

Ruth was a Moabite who married an Israelite who had come to Moab seeking relief from famine with his family. After her husband's death, Ruth chose to return with her Mother-in-law, Naomi to Israel and care for her. With no men for support, Ruth worked hard gleaning in the fields for food. She humbly accepted Naomi's advice and customs, even a marriage that would provide for them. Professing a faith in God, Ruth was part of the bloodline of Jesus.

DAY 11

Ruth—Humble

Ruth 2:11-12, *Boaz replied, "I've been told all about what you have done for your mother-in-law since the death of your husband—how you left your father and mother and your homeland and came to live with a people you did not know before. May the Lord repay you for what you have done. May you be richly rewarded by the Lord, the God of Israel, under whose wings you have come to take refuge."*

Heavenly Father, scripture tells us that You oppose the proud but show favor to the humble (James 4:6). Many times pride has gotten in my way and caused me problems. It's so easy to compare myself to others and be in competition with them. Our society seems to favor the proud and successful. But that is not Your way of thinking.

Help me turn away from selfish ambition and vain conceit. In dealing with others, help me be less self-centered and more God-centered in the way I treat people, make decisions, and respond to circumstances. Show me how to walk away from pride, arrogance, conceitedness, and that attitude of superiority that so easily entangles me.

Do not let me think more highly of myself than I ought (Romans 12:3), or that I'm too good to do any task. But let me walk humbly, even taking on the role of a servant for others. Let me look to the needs of others and value them, submitting to the authorities You have placed in my life, whether legal, governmental, those I work or minister with and even family members.

When I make a mistake, prompt me to respond with humility and repentance, asking forgiveness when necessary and making amends. And when there is victory in my life show me how to celebrate with humility, giving rightful praise and honor to You and not myself.

I bow before You and seek to obey Your will. I am humbled by Your power, Your sovereignty, Your authority.

Father, strengthen my character to be like Ruth: Humble

Read more about Ruth: the book of Ruth

Hannah poured out her heart to God
in her anguished and earnest prayer for a
son. And trusting in God's answer, made
a sincere vow to return the blessing to Him.
As hard as that was, she rejoiced greatly in
God's provision to her and praised God
in prayer. And stayed true to her vow.

DAY 12

Hannah—Earnest

1 Samuel 1:10-11, *In her deep anguish Hannah prayed to the Lord, weeping bitterly. And she made a vow, saying, "Lord Almighty, if you will only look on your servant's misery and remember me, and not forget your servant but give her a son, then I will give him to the Lord for all the days of his life.*

Heavenly Father, there is much in the world to be heartbroken over: illness, abuse, death, loss, poverty, political disunity, injustice. And You know the desires of my heart as You knew Hannah's. I will not give up, but earnestly pray, pouring out my feelings and heartaches to You, and trusting in Your answers, Your timing to meet my needs.

There is so much in my life that is beyond my control. Yet even when there is no hope from the world, and I cannot see a way out or through, there is nothing too difficult for You. I cry out to You for answers, for understanding, for strength to cope with my circumstances. As I pour out my heart, my faith is in You. Give me wisdom, give me vision.

When I see the good of what's happening in my life, I earnestly give You the thanks and praise. It is You who give life and take it away, You who send poverty and wealth. You who heal and save. I will rejoice with a sincere heart over all You do for me, acknowledging that every blessing comes from You.

Help me also, be true to my word and faithful to my promises, no matter how hard it is. Like Hannah, I need to hold Your blessings loosely enough so I don't love them more than I love You. Do not let me make rash vows, or promises without thinking them through. There is no bargaining with You - let my yes mean yes and my no mean no. It is not by my strength that I prevail.

Father, strengthen my character to be like Hannah: Earnest in prayer and keeping my promises to You. Amen

Read more about Hannah: 1 Samuel 1:1-2:11

Samuel was Hannah's son, God's answer to her prayer. She gave him to the Priest Eli to be raised in the Lord's house. Samuel was the last judge of Israel and the first Prophet after Moses. Although he lived among people who did not honor the Lord, Samuel interceded for the people. He was instrumental in subduing the Philistines and set up the Ebenezer Stone to commemorate it. He taught the Israelites to turn from idolatry and worship only the Lord. He served in obedience to God, and anointed Saul first, and then David as Israel's kings.

DAY 13

Samuel—Honorable

1 Samuel 3:19, *The Lord was with Samuel as he grew up, and he let none of Samuel's words fall to the ground.*

Heavenly Father, refine my heart. Enable my eyes, my ears to see You at work. To hear Your voice, to feel Your presence. Help me grow in awareness that You are with me wherever I go. And let that be a powerful deterrent to keep me behaving honorably. Let it also be an awesome reassurance that You see my honorable way of living.

When I hear Your voice, let my response be as Samuel's: "Speak, Lord, for your servant is listening" (1 Samuel 3:11). Let me honor You with my attitudes, words, actions, and time. It's so easy to get busy and put spiritual disciplines aside. Help me prioritize those things that honor You. Not only reading Your Word and saying a quick prayer, but like Samuel, show me how to make time to also listen for Your voice when I pray, seek You in worship, fast when I need Your direction. If not from food, then from some behavior or influence in my life.

Like Samuel, I also live among people who do not honor You or live by godly standards. Remind me to set up "Ebenezers" to mark Your presence and influence in my life. As You reveal Yourself to me and Your purpose for my life, let Your words sink deep into my spirit. Let them take root in my life and be the foundation for all I do.

Like Samuel, let me grow in stature and in favor with You and with others (1 Samuel 2:26).

Father, strengthen my character to be like Samuel: Honorable. Amen

Read more about Samuel: 1 Samuel 2:18-26; 3:1-19; 7

David was the youngest son of Jesse and watched over the family's flocks of sheep. When hearing of the disrespectful attack by Goliath the Philistine, he accepted personal responsibility to do something about it. He was confident You would fight for and through him and bring victory—which he gave You the credit for before the battle. He became King of Israel and was part of the bloodline of Jesus.

DAY 14

David—Confident

1 Samuel 17:40; 45-46, *Then he [David] took his staff in his hand, chose five smooth stones from the stream, put them in the pouch of his shepherd's bag and, with his sling in his hand, approached the Philistine. Saying...I come against you in the name of the Lord Almighty...This day the Lord will deliver you into my hands...and the whole world will know that there is a God in Israel.*

Heavenly Father, there are times I feel like the underdog. When I am overwhelmed give me confidence like David to take on the enemies I face. When I come up against trouble:

1—Help me look beyond myself and be confident in Your perspective, recognizing when an affront is also someone or something in defiance of You. Looking only at myself limits the scope of solutions I can see and perform. But an offense to You makes it Your battle. Like David, I don't have to fear defeat when You are in the fight with me.

2—Help me trust that You have already prepared me for the battle. I know You have brought circumstances into my life that teach and prepare me for whatever is to come. Intentionally and purposefully You have given me spiritual gifts, talents, abilities and experiences to make me who I am. Like David, show me how to use those things instead of feeling I need to conform to what others expect of me. Give me confidence in Your preparation for whatever battle I face.

3—Let me voice confidence in You, giving You the glory for the victory even before it happens! Sometimes I try and do things quietly so if I fail it won't reflect badly on You. Father, let my fear diminish and my faith grow!

With all that's happening in the world today, and in my own circumstances, help me look beyond myself to all You can do in and with and through me. I trust in Your preparation and Your purposefulness for my life. And in Your victory.

Father, strengthen my character to be like David: Confident. Amen

Read more about David: 1 Samuel 17 - 2 Samuel 12

Reflections

Two weeks - way to go!! Are you finding a rhythm in your schedule for prayer?
> If you have been able to be consistent in praying this week – Great job!
>
> If you got off track, make a plan to remedy that and just pick up where you left off.

During your prayer time this week, what has God shown you about Himself?

_____

> About yourself?

_____

In thinking back over the prayers this week...
> Which of the characteristics would you say already describe you? Think of an example of when you demonstrated that trait.

_____

_____

_____

> Did any of the characters or characteristics stand out to you? Why?

_____

Do you know what your Spiritual Gifts are? Every believer has one or more. And they may change over time. List what they are and how you are using them.

> If you don't have an opportunity to use them now, ask God to show you where and when.

> If you don't know what your gifts are, consider taking a Spiritual Gifts test to find out. Your church or a trusted Christian website are good places to look.

Joshua, Caleb, Rahab, and David are all strong characters who found strength in their faith to go forward in the presence of fear and oppression of different kinds. Have there been times in the past when you faced social, political or physical oppression and had to stand your ground?

_____

_____

Or have you observed others facing overwhelming odds they conquered?
    What did that look like?

_____

_____

    What obstacles do you face today that you need God's strength to overcome? Write them here and ask for His presence and wisdom to guide you to be a bold, courageous and confident conqueror.

_____

_____

It's so easy to put ourselves first. But God's economy is different. Ask God to show you if there are times you have been prideful, arrogant, self-serving. And if so, to show you the way to be humble, caring for others. Even Jesus set the example in washing His disciples' feet. Look for places you can serve others to take on that quality. If any come to mind, list them here:

_____

_____

_____

Hannah and Samuel came to the Lord in humility and earnestness. Pour out your heart before the Lord. And be responsive to His reply. Write what you hear Him saying to you.

David's Fighting Men came from the twelve Tribes of Israel
to support and extend David's kingship over all
the land the Lord had promised. They were skilled
in weapons and in fighting and were loyal to David.
They were mighty and honorable and fought
and won many battles with the Lord's help.

DAY 15

David's Fighting Men—Ready to act

1 Chronicles 12: 8, 23, 38, *They were brave warriors, ready for battle and able to handle the shield and spear… armed for battle … fighting men who volunteered to serve in the ranks.*

Heavenly Father, I want to be loyal to You in the good times as well as in the times of challenge and trials. I need to be prepared for battle and ready for action as David's men were. Not on a military battlefield, but armed with weapons and ready to fight the mental, emotional, social, relational and spiritual battles I find myself in.

Teach me through prayer to put on and use the armor You give in Ephesians 6:10-18

I put on the Helmet of Salvation to protect and direct my thoughts, guide and guard my mind, and all that comes into or goes out from my head. Help me make godly decisions about what I see, hear, taste, smell, but also what comes out.

Father, help me focus on things that are good and pure and godly. Keep me clear of fear, doubts, insecurity, or unworthiness. When those thoughts come, I won't dwell on them but remember my identity comes from the truth of who You say I am: a child of God, chosen, holy and dearly loved (Colossians 3:12).

Don't let me be led astray by the temptations the world pitches at me, or by sin the evil one entices me with. Protect my mind, and thoughts.

I wear the Breastplate of Righteousness as my chest protector. Your Righteousness forms a protective cover that stops darts and arrows and deflects blows. Allow it to fend off weapons that come into my personal range or space so that I'm not harmed.

Let me not be bothered by other people's words or attitudes. Let no personal or professional attacks find their target in me. My circumstances will not defeat me, but I will rise to fight back, unharmed.

Tying the Belt of Truth around my waist helps me see and discern truth from lies. I don't want to base my attitudes or decisions in life on deceptions, misinformation, half-truths, or lies. It helps me recognize truth when I hear

it. And helps me speak it so I don't try to sway others by exaggeration or deceptive talk. Father, in my relationships, my business dealings, finances, health issues and spiritual concerns, help me seek and recognize truth. And walk in it.

I step into the Shoes of the Gospel of peace, saying I am ready to go, ready to accept Your marching orders. Guide me and light my way so I can see the direction You want me to go. Show me how to overcome obstacles in my path so I don't stumble or turn my ankle. And let me leave behind goodness and mercy in the circumstances and with the people I encounter.

I pick up my Shield of Faith and hold it up to stand behind it. It protects myself and my loved ones from the onslaught of attacks that come our way from the world and the evil one. Let it repel flaming arrows, grenades, whatever is launched at us by the world or the evil one, meaning unfortunate circumstances, illness, the frustrations and challenges of an imperfect world.

    Linking shields with others of faith forms a wall of support and protection. Show me who I can link with in prayer. Alone or together, our shields of faith can push forward and advance against the enemy. I can go forward in faith into circumstances without fear, standing up for what is right.

I take up my Sword of the Spirit which is the Word of God, the Bible. Let me use Your Word to inflict harm on the enemy, standing my ground and defending it with scripture. I will fight to preserve what You have given me.

    When lies are spoken I can combat them with truth in scripture: about my worth, my identity, Your faithfulness and sovereignty and power.

    When tempted I can rely on scriptures about Your promise to strengthen me and defeat the devil.

    When discouraged or depressed I will recall verses that tell me to put my hope in You and not to fear.

    These Words stab at the enemy, to harm and defeat them. And give me courage to stay in the fight.

Father, strengthen my character like David's Fighting Men: Ready to act. Amen

    Read more about David's Fighting Men: 1 Chronicles 11-12
    Read more about Spiritual Armor: Ephesians 6:10-18

Each tribe was named for a son of Jacob and was made up of the descendants of that son. The twelve tribes of Israel are part of Jewish identity and the fulfillment of God's promise to Abraham, Isaac and Jacob to make their descendants as numerous as the stars (Genesis 15:5). Each tribe was given a prophetic blessing by Jacob before he died and given parcels of land when they reached the Promised Land. Of those who fought bravely with David, these men stood out from the tribe of Issachar.

DAY 16

Men of Issachar—Discerning

1 Chronicles 12:32, *from Issachar, men who understood the times and knew what Israel should do—200 chiefs, with all their relatives under their command*

Heavenly Father, make me like the men of Issachar. They were experiencing confusing times as Saul had died in battle and David was the new King. Israel had only ever had one king. And there were still military enemies of Israel.

My days are so confusing and filled with disinformation. There is great political and social unrest, financial instability and worldwide disasters. It's hard to discern what is true and what is false. People in positions of authority have abused their power, taking advantage of others and even causing great harm. And some of the media seems to have lost its loyalty to the truth as well.

With so many things seen as permissible now, it's hard to hold on to godly values. Strengthen me to live my life and make my decisions from a Biblical perspective. Give me insight into the political, national, and global issues and wisdom to understand the agendas behind the movements going on in my world today. Help me see the truth of things. Teach me to understand how to follow You and show me how to respond rightly whether in the national realm, my community or in my business and personal life.

Father, strengthen my character to be like the Men of Issachar: Discerning, with a knowledge and understanding of how to live in these times. Amen

Read more about the Men of Issachar: 1 Chronicles 12:19-40

In one short chapter we see an amazing example of wisdom, bravery and diplomacy from the least expected place. It almost reads...like a fairy tale. A wealthy but mean man married a beautiful and intelligent woman, Abigail. King David's men did this man a favor, but in return, were rebuked, disrespected and sent away. In response, David returned to destroy this foolish man and all his people. Uh-oh! Abigail acted quickly, boldly, and diplomatically. Following her husband's untimely death, our heroine also married the king.

DAY 17

Abigail—Diplomatic

1 Samuel 25:17-18, *Now think it over and see what you can do, because disaster is hanging over our master and his whole household... Abigail acted quickly.*

Heavenly Father, in a similar situation I can think of many other options I might have turned to.

I might have sat down and wept, bemoaning the fact that all would be destroyed because of someone else's short-sighted foolishness. Maybe have a well-deserved pity-party over my impending demise, leaving me a victim of calamity.

Or given the person responsible a piece of my mind in a belittling tirade. Or demanded they fight to defend me. Or try to make a legal argument, citing no contractual agreement had been made. Or packed up and left, leaving the others to be killed.

Father, my thoughts are not as wise or as noble or diplomatic as Abigail's. Thank You for this example of someone who did not act out of helplessness, or anger, or self-righteousness, or fear. It seems as if she must have been directed by You.

Keep my spiritual ears open when I feel up against a wall. Especially in difficult or challenging circumstances let me consider my options with a clear head. Guide my thoughts quickly to what is appropriate, diplomatic, and will save the ones around me. Help me think through and act quickly with a wise solution.

Father, strengthen my character to be like Abigail: Diplomatic, especially when so much is on the line. Amen

Read more about Abigail: 1 Samuel 25

Solomon, David's son, ruled Israel for 40 years. He supervised the building of the Temple and ruled with great wisdom given to him by God. In a dream, God offered Solomon whatever he wanted. And because he did not ask for wealth or long life or political victory, God gave him wisdom to rule, discernment in justice that was world-renowned. He wrote Proverbs, Ecclesiastes and Song of Solomon.

DAY 18

Solomon—Wise

1 Kings 4:29-34, *God gave Solomon wisdom and very great insight, and a breadth of understanding as measureless as the sand on the seashore. Solomon's wisdom was greater than the wisdom of all the people of the East, and greater than all the wisdom of Egypt. He was wiser than anyone else, including Ethan the Ezrahite—wiser than Heman, Kalkol and Darda, the sons of Mahol. And his fame spread to all the surrounding nations. He spoke three thousand proverbs and his songs numbered a thousand and five. He spoke about plant life, from the cedar of Lebanon to the hyssop that grows out of walls. He also spoke about animals and birds, reptiles and fish. From all nations people came to listen to Solomon's wisdom, sent by all the kings of the world, who had heard of his wisdom.*

Heavenly Father, Solomon recognized the enormity of both the blessing and the responsibility You had given him as king. And in the face of this, and in humility, he asked for wisdom. I too, acknowledge Your faithfulness to me and the incredible blessing You have poured out on my life. And like Solomon, I also feel very inadequate to fill the needs of the people in my life. On my own, I cannot do it.

I am often faced with opposing views and don't know how to handle the disagreement. In a famous example of Solomon ruling wisely, he discerned that the true mother of the living baby would give it up rather than see it destroyed. Help me see past the loudest voice or the squeakiest wheel to the heart of the matter at hand. Give me insight and wisdom to know what is true and what is not.

Give me a discerning heart to speak to and relate to those You bring into my life. Help me distinguish between right and wrong and be able to speak the truth in love into their lives as I live according to Your guidance. Show me when to speak and when to keep silent. Show me how to share the understanding You have given me when it comes to teaching and encouraging others.

Father, strengthen my character to be like Solomon: Wise. Amen

Read more about Solomon: 1 Kings 3-11

Jehoshaphat was a good King of Judah who followed the Lord, removing idol worship and providing priests who took the Book of the Law of the Lord throughout the towns in Judah to teach the people. When confronted with a vast army coming against him, his first response was to proclaim a fast and pray, seeking God's wisdom and trusting God for his defense.

DAY 19

Jehoshaphat—Trusting God

2 Chronicles 20:6-12, , *"O Lord, God of my fathers, are You not the God who is in heaven? You rule over all the kingdoms of the nations. Power and might are in Your hand, and no one can withstand You. I stand in Your presence... and will cry out to You in our distress, and You will hear us and save us... For we have no power to face this vast army that is attacking us. We do not know what to do, but our eyes are upon You!"*

Heavenly Father, I want to trust You have the answers I need, and seek You out when I have decisions to make. Jehoshaphat heard so-called prophets telling other kings only good predictions. Don't let me fall for or be led astray by someone who just says what they think I want to hear. I will seek Your counsel and honor it above all others.

And when hardships come, lead me to fast and pray rather than respond with anxiousness, confusion, anger, frustration, or discouragement. Don't let me be satisfied with finding people who will agree with whatever position I take, adding to the confusion. I don't want to simply "lean on my own understanding" but want to "trust in You with all my heart" (Proverbs 3:5).

I acknowledge my insufficiency and affirm my faith and trust in You. If I look at You instead of the problem, my focus stays positive. And if I can see the problem through Your perspective that changes everything!

Father, I feel more courageous when I connect with and focus on You: singing praise music, praying out loud, walking in Your Creation. You empower me. When I don't know what to do, I will put my eyes on You.

Father, strengthen my character to be like Jehoshaphat: Trusting God. Amen

Read more about Jehoshaphat: 2 Chronicles 17-20

Hezekiah was a good king (few and far between) of the Northern kingdom of Judah, and reigned as king from age 25 to 54. His father was King Ahab (one of the worst kings) who was married to Jezebel, and led the people to worship Baal and other idols. Even with these wicked beginnings, Hezekiah removed the high places that other kings had allowed to be used for pagan worship and smashed all the sacred stones and Asherah poles.
He reopened and rededicated the Temple in Jerusalem.
And he was a powerful pray-er.

DAY 20

Hezekiah—Powerful Pray-er

2 Kings 19:15, *"Lord, the God of Israel, enthroned between the cherubim, you alone are God over all the kingdoms of the earth. You have made heaven and earth. Give ear, Lord, and hear; open your eyes Lord, and see, listen to the words Sennacherib has sent to ridicule the living God."*

Heavenly Father, my loved ones and I may not have to do battle on horseback with spears like Hezekiah, but our enemies are real. Powers and forces come against my family, my godly values, my emotions, finances, and life circumstances, all trying to defeat me and make me lose my faith in You.

Sometimes these enemies are of the world so I need to gain Your perspective on my circumstances and seek Your solutions to the problems I face.

Sometimes I am my own worst enemy, and I need to be reminded that You made me in Your image, wonderfully and purposefully. I need Your help to silence the negative and critical voices in my head and listen in prayer for Your voice more.

And sometimes the enemy is a spiritual one, seeking to harm, kill and destroy. I need to mount a prayerful offense. Thank You that You give me spiritual armor so I can be protected and fight against these enemies as well. And stand firm in my faith.

Father, thank You that there is nothing too big and nothing too small for me to bring to You in prayer. Remind me to bring my personal struggles to You. My professional and financial concerns. My relationship difficulties. My health issues. Whether an overwhelming situation or a seemingly insignificant detail, teach me how to pray effectively and powerfully.

You have the authority and power to act in all circumstances. Thank You that You also possess the desire to answer my prayers. You can do immeasurably more than I can ask or even imagine in my life and in the lives of my loved ones. I give You the glory!

Father, strengthen my character to be like Hezekiah: a Powerful Pray-er. Amen

Read more about Hezekiah: 2 Kings 18:17-19:37

When King Josiah was 26, he set to repair the Temple and the Book of the Law was found. When it was read to him, he responded by weeping and tearing his robes and humbling himself before God. He committed wholly to it and brought the people back to worshipping the Lord, removing and burning all altars and items of idol worship.

DAY 21

Josiah—Responsive

2 Kings 22:1-2, *Josiah was eight years old when he became king, and he reigned in Jerusalem thirty-one years...He did what was right in the eyes of the Lord and followed completely the ways of his father David, not turning aside to the right or to the left.*

Heavenly Father let me be responsive to, and deeply touched by Your Word. Let it have an effect on me that will humble me and call me to recommit to worshipping You alone. The next time I read scripture, show me not only what it says, but what it means and what it means to me, in my life. Let me even recall now the last scripture I read...or the last time what I read really impacted me.

Give me a hunger to hear from You. Show me how to make time in my schedule to read the Bible regularly. When I read Your Word make its meaning clear to me, profoundly affecting my thoughts, attitudes, beliefs, relationships and actions. Silence any other voices I hear, especially from the world or my flesh or the evil one. And let me immediately obey what the Bible says.

Your Word, the Bible, written so long ago, still has relevance in my time. Help me read it, study to understand it, and watch for ways it applies to my life. If I misunderstand, let me hear Your voice correcting me. If I forget to obey, remind me. And if I don't want to obey, change my attitude.

Father, let me know Your Word so intimately it becomes my strength and my guide. Let me be eager to speak boldly of my relationship with You to encourage others.

Father, strengthen my character to be like Josiah: Responsive to You, and Your Word. Amen

Read more about Josiah: 2 Kings 22-23

Reflections

You are more than halfway through this 40 day journey! AWESOME!!
We are cheering you on!!
If you have been able to be consistent in praying this week—good for you!
If you got off track, make a plan to remedy that and just pick up where you left off.
During your prayer time this week, what has God shown you about Himself?

    About yourself?

In thinking back over the prayers this week...
    Which of the characteristics would you say already describe you? Think of an example of when you demonstrated that trait.

_____

_____

    Did any of the characters or characteristics stand out to you? Why?

_____

At this point: Any breakthroughs?
Any fun examples of a new character trait springing up in your life and behavior, maybe when you least expected it?

_____

David's men and Abigail were ready when the battle came upon them. Is there something going on or coming up in your life that you need discernment, diplomacy or wisdom about? List those things here and bring them before God one at a time. Listen for His direction as you seek His guidance and write out anything you hear from Him.

If praying on the Spiritual Armor is something new to you, read more about it in the Appendix. And consider making it part of your daily prayer routine. We can't always know in advance when an attack or challenge will come, so being prepared and armed is important.

When under attack, Jehoshaphat and Hezekiah trusted God over any other power that their flesh or the world could offer. If you feel under attack, physically, emotionally, financially, mentally, relationally or spiritually, seek God's counsel in scripture and in prayer. Ask for a vision or revelation. Fast for a time. Fasting can be from food or other things. Check out the Appendix for more information on fasting.

Pray Jehoshaphat and Hezekiah's prayers from scripture, putting in your own name and name your specific enemy or need. Consider writing your prayers out. And write down the result of your prayers. Things may change, or may not. They may resolve as you expect or in some unforeseen way. Maybe the circumstances don't change, but you or your perspective do.

When was the last time you read scripture and let it actually move you like Josiah? Encourage you? Change you?
What was that scripture?

_____

_____

Set aside some quiet time this week with the intention of reading your Bible until it speaks to you. Let God's Word encourage you about something you're facing. Or give you discernment on an issue. Let it give you wisdom, or move you to act. Or just shine a light of clarity on something you never noticed or understood before.
Write the scripture that impacted you here, and how you responded to it.

_____

_____

Halfway point check:

Have you sensed any pushback?
	When you are praying intentionally and consistently, that does not make the evil one happy. You may sense pushback in finding yourself facing hardship or discouragement. Or there could be an upset with a relationship, or your work or home life. Maybe a sudden health issue or unexplained crisis. It may seem to come out of the blue, with no warning and no logic as to why things are happening.
Have you experienced anything like that? What?

_____
_____
_____
_____
_____
_____

If this happens it could be spiritual, so it's helpful to be sure you are praying on Armor of God as part of your daily prayer time. Even a simple prayer like:
Heavenly Father, thank You for the armor You give me that protects me as I pray. I put on the Helmet of Salvation to protect my mind, and the Breastplate of Righteousness as a protective cover for my heart. I put on the Belt of Truth to help me discern truth and reject any lies. I wear the Shoes of the Gospel of Peace and take up the Shield of Faith and the sword of the Spirit to fight in the battles You call me to.
For more information see the Resource Guide on Spiritual Armor for Battle in the Appendix at the back of the book. Page 102

And ask God to guard you and protect you, your family, your health, finances, relationships, home, job, and whatever else you feel led to pray about that could be attacked. Ask God to keep you standing firm.

It also helps to talk with another Christian friend and ask them to pray for you and what you're experiencing. Or even for the duration of this commitment.

All his life, Daniel held tightly to his faith, his beliefs about God and his convictions about how to live a godly life. He did so as a young man in the midst of being kidnapped and taken a thousand miles away from home. At 35, Daniel refused to worship a gold image of King Nebuchadnezzar, enduring being thrown into a fiery furnace for his conviction to God. And at 85, in the face of evil plots and being thrown into a den of hungry lions, he still worshipped and prayed to only God.

DAY 22

Daniel—Dedicated

Daniel 6:26-27, *"For he is the living God and he endures forever; his kingdom will not be destroyed, his dominion will never end. He rescues and he saves; he performs signs and wonders in the heavens and on the earth. He has rescued Daniel from the power of the lions."*

Heavenly Father, help me persevere and be dedicated to living out my faith my whole life. Let me be consistent in prayer and worship, recognizing that You are the only One worthy of my worship and dedication no matter the social or political climate.

Wherever I am in life, there is opportunity to live a life dedicated to You like Daniel:

> As a young person—Inexperienced and being far away from home and the support of family, it is easy to be led astray by the lure of the world and its values. Strengthen me not to give in to temptation and sin, or the social pressures that abound. Help me see the "hook" beneath the tempting lure that would draw me away from godly living.
>
> In the middle ages—Strengthen me to live the way You have taught me and not to give in to the pressures or temptations of whatever society offers or tells me I deserve or should do. It's easy to want to go along to get along or "keep up with the Joneses." Help me behave according to my convictions in the face of social pressure or staying in my "comfort zone."
>
> In the senior years—Old age, frailty and fatigue can make us easy targets for temptation just to sit back and enjoy "the good life." Let me still hear Your voice and be quick to obey, even when opposition or powers may come against me. Help me use my circumstances, even retirement, to find ways to honor You in all the stages of my life.

I want to be faithful in prayer, trusting in You throughout my whole life. Bolster my efforts in living out my spiritual convictions, so I can be a person of integrity and faith: prayerful, trustworthy, honest, honorable.

Father, strengthen my character to be like Daniel: Dedicated to living my whole life for You. Amen

Read more about Daniel: Daniel 1-6

Ezra was a Hebrew Priest and Scribe at the end of Israel's seventy-year Babylonian captivity. He was chosen to bring people and valuable items, silver and gold and supplies back to Jerusalem for the rebuilding of the Temple. He didn't ask for military escort in order to show his faith and trust in You for protection, and he knew that actions speak louder than words. Ezra knew and lived his life according to the Law of Moses, and taught it to all the returned exiles.

DAY 23
Ezra—Authentic

Ezra 7:10; 8:21-23, *Ezra had devoted himself to the study and observance of the Law of the Lord, and to teaching its decrees and laws in Israel.*
There, by the Ahava Canal, I proclaimed a fast, so that we might humble ourselves before our God and ask him for a safe journey for us and our children, with all our possessions. I was ashamed to ask the king for soldiers and horsemen to protect us from enemies... So we fasted and petitioned our God about this, and he answered our prayer.

Heavenly Father, I wonder what my actions say to others around me about my faith in You.
When I seem afraid and worried over circumstances, does that show others I don't really trust Your protection and provision? Help me show my faith in You in my responses when things are going well, and in difficult times. When things don't go my way, remind me that You are in control, and that You have my back!

There is absolutely nothing that can happen to me that You don't know about. And I believe that You filter everything that comes to me, through Your fingers of love. Even in the bad times, You have prepared me, and You are with me. And have promised to never, ever leave me.

Whatever is happening, remind me to focus my attention and energy on You. I can turn to You in prayer, in praise, in pain, or in frustration, even anger. You can handle it all. I can find encouragement and direction in Your Word, the Bible. Knowing what I believe is a start, but living like I am truly depending on You for direction and protection can be challenging.

As Ezra did, help me live according to Your Word even when it is not convenient for me. Even when I must make changes in my behavior to match what I say I believe. Let me be authentic by walking the walk I talk. Get my attention when I need correction or am not behaving like I should.

Father, strengthen my character to be like Ezra: Authentic, in my words and actions. Amen

Read more about Ezra: Ezra 7-10; Nehemiah 8

Nehemiah, a Jewish leader living in Babylon after the exile, was cup bearer to the king. Upon hearing of the condition of the wall around Jerusalem, he was heartbroken. Through prayer and fasting, the Lord gave him favor with the king who sent him to Jerusalem to rebuild the wall. Facing all kinds of opposition and even political and military attack, he remained calm and self-controlled, working his plan, and modeled trusting God for the work to be completed.

DAY 24

Nehemiah—Self-Controlled

Nehemiah 4:13, 16-18, *Therefore I stationed some of the people behind the lowest points of the wall at the exposed places, posting them by families, with their swords, spears and bows... From that day on, half of my men did the work, while the other half were equipped with spears, shields, bows and armor... Those who carried materials did their work with one hand and held a weapon in the other, and each of the builders wore his sword at his side as he worked.*

Heavenly Father, with wisdom, Nehemiah made his inspections in secret and only revealed his purpose when he had a plan. Help me not run ahead of myself with enthusiasm until I am ready to work a plan. Like You did with Nehemiah, show me the order to accomplish any goals You give me. And bring the manpower needed with the organization to coordinate it.

Like Nehemiah, when I face opposition, remind me to come to You. Teach me how to pivot when I need to make a change of plans. And remind me to stay strong in my faith for spiritual encouragement—and not be overwhelmed by enemies.

Another of his challenges came from within. But Nehemiah was able to change social and financial behaviors to allow a successful solution involving workers and their families, priests, nobles and officials. Help me overcome my anger and emotional reactions to problems and find solutions that work. And give me favor with people of influence to bring the solution about.

Over and over again, problems that could have defeated his great purpose if Nehemiah had stopped everything to fight back, were solved as he demonstrated self-control and countered the attacks with prayer, inspiration and steady work.

In my life, many things frustrate me. And problems arise that bring me to anger and can lead to unwise actions—in business, my relationships, health, and personal issues. Remind me to come to You with my problems. Help me take control over my reactions and discouragement. Give me Your wisdom to find creative solutions and the ability to see them through.

Father, strengthen my character to be like Nehemiah: Self-Controlled. Amen

Read more about Nehemiah: Nehemiah 1-6:16

Esther was a Jewish orphan raised by her uncle Mordecai in post-captivity Babylon. Beautiful, she was taken to the palace and King Xerxes made her his Queen. Her heritage hidden, she found herself in a significant position to impact the survival of the Jews. She risked it all to expose the evil plot to the king and save her people.

DAY 25

Esther—Risk-Taker

Esther 4:14, *And who knows but that you [Esther] have come to your royal position for such a time as this?"*

Heavenly Father, thank You for Your promises to always be with me and never leave me. Thank You that I can look at my own past and see where You have provided for me in circumstances. that were hard, challenging, scary. Although no one has ever threatened my life or family like Esther, I know the difficulties I face are a concern of Yours. And I know there is no problem too big for You to handle, and no problem too small for You to help me with.

If there is something You are preparing me for or calling me to, open my eyes to see it. And give me the courage to act. It may not be as big or as risky as Esther's call. It may only be something small: inviting someone to church, praying with a friend or stranger, reaching out to help someone.

Father, is there something You have orchestrated in my life that I need to respond to, because You have placed me where I am *"for such a time as this?"*

Help me see where and how You could use me. Don't let me do it in my own strength, but like Esther, let me go forward in prayer and in Your power.

Father, strengthen my character to be like Esther: a Risk-Taker. Amen

Read more about Esther: book of Esther

Job, it is said, feared God and shunned evil, was blameless and upright. The devil, who received permission from God to strike at him, took his flocks, herds, children, servants, and health. Yet Job did not curse God but humbled himself recognizing God's sovereignty and power. God blessed Job even more in his later life

DAY 26

Job—God-fearing

Job 1:21-22, *"Naked I came from my mother's womb, and naked I will depart. The Lord gave and the Lord has taken away; may the name of the Lord be praised." In all this, Job did not sin by charging God with wrongdoing.*

Heavenly Father, I have often wondered why You singled out Job and allowed so much suffering to come into one life. How tragic, and yet how strong was his faith that it stood up to all the devil threw at him. What a testimony that he could still praise You in the face of all the tragedy and suffering.

It makes me wonder if I have made comfort and ease idols?

Father, my life is so blessed. With so much. And I take so much of it for granted. Help me be more aware of and thankful for all You have given me.

There have been times in my life when I had opportunities to see what You have created or done and been in total awe of You: the vastness of the ocean, the power of a hurricane, the immenseness of mountains, and looking through a powerful telescope to see the explosions of light in a nebula star nursery that we only perceive with our eyes as a tiny bright spot in the sky at night.

I have a reverence and respect for Your immense power, Your infinite creativity of the universe and all that's in it. And Your ability to be everywhere at all times, knowing every human being on the planet and their minds and hearts, needs and desires, blows me away.

I will never tire of being amazed by You. Like Job, I am unworthy of Your attention, Your blessing, Your love. And yet all that I enjoy in my life and in my relationship with You comes from being blessed and loved and cared for, by You. Your love transcends my unworthiness. Your faithfulness trumps my undeserving state.

Forgive me when I throw accusations at You or question Your goodness or purpose. In the good times and bad, I stand in awe of You, in humble and respectful adoration. That translates as fearing You. You tell me that "the fear of the Lord is the beginning of wisdom" (Psalm 111:10). And I seek to be wise.

Father, strengthen my character to be like Job, God-fearing. Amen

Read more about Job: 1-2; 42:7-17

Habakkuk was a prophet who saw the injustice of the wicked prospering and questioned You, remaining hopeful in even the direst of circumstances. He wrote down his conversation with You and asked for You to repeat Your deeds of awe so the people would revere and worship You.

DAY 27

Habakkuk—Hopeful

Habakkuk 3:17-18, *Though the fig tree does not bud and there are no grapes on the vines, though the olive crop fails and the fields produce no food, though there are no sheep in the pen and no cattle in the stalls, yet I will rejoice in the Lord, I will be joyful in God my Savior.*
Habakkuk 3:1-2, *Lord, I have heard of your fame; I stand in awe of your deeds, Lord. Repeat them in our day, in our time make them known; in wrath remember mercy.*

Heavenly Father, in my day, I also see wickedness and wrongdoing triumphing over justice. There is destruction and violence, conflict and strife. And I echo Habakkuk's words: How long before You make such a display of Your power that none can deny You? Till everyone in the world sees what I see in You? And bows down and praises Your name?

With the state of the world right now, THIS would be the perfect time for You to show Yourself and Your mighty deeds. There are people in the world who are unaware of Your existence. And others who have heard, but deny Your mighty power and true identity as the One True God. In this day and age, let us see Your splendor and power! I wait for the day of Your return. I praise You Father, and I stand ready and hopeful to see You act!

I believe in You because of who You are and because of Your mighty deeds. Just in my life, I recognize and acknowledge the ways You have delivered me, protected me, provided for me, comforted me. But on a larger scale, You could demonstrate Your power to the whole world! You could impact the entire planet and prove Your existence and sovereignty. As they hear of Your fame, they would stand in awe of You.

Yet even if You choose not to act as I want in my lifetime, I will still trust in You. I will rejoice and be glad in You. I have hope because You are my strength who will enable me to survive, cope, and thrive.

Father, strengthen my character to be like Habakkuk: forever Hopeful.
Amen

Read more about Habakkuk: Habakkuk 1-3

Mary was a young virgin, visited by an angel who delivered the miraculous news that she would be the mother of Jesus, the long-awaited Savior of the world! Although taken completely by surprise, and not completely understanding how this would happen, she accepted and rejoiced in God's purpose for her life.

DAY 28

Mary—Joyful

Luke 1:46-49, *And Mary said: "My soul glorifies the Lord and my spirit rejoices in God my Savior, for he has been mindful of the humble state of his servant. From now on all generations will call me blessed, the Mighty One has done great things for me—holy is his name."*

Heavenly Father, help me have joy in Your plan for my life. Even if it's not what I might choose for myself. Don't let me base my sense of joy simply on having comfortable circumstances and a trouble-free life. I may not be happy in my situation, but there is transcendent joy when Your plan is the dominant influence in my life and I am able to fulfill a godly purpose.

Sometimes I cannot make sense of the twists and turns my life takes. There are times I don't know whether to stay or go, wait or act. I can't see how things will play out, so I make a plan. And many times switch to Plan B, or Plan C, or D, or E, F...

But You have the perspective of eternity. You have answered my prayers in far better ways than I could have asked for or even imagined. You can make a way when I can't see a way. And I can trust that being Your handiwork, I have been created for works which You have prepared in advance for me (Ephesians 2:10). And to the extent I can rise to those, I will have joy.

Like Mary, let me sing songs to You and praise You, for who You are and for the things You have done. Knowing Your love for me is great, and that You are trustworthy, and faithful, I can be joyful in all You have planned for me.

So regardless of my momentary discomforts, let me find joy each day. Help me look past whatever tries to produce anxiety in me, and be filled with Your peace and presence. Remind me to rejoice in being Your child. And in every blessing You have poured out on me.

Father, strengthen my character to be like Mary: Joyful. Amen

Read more about Mary: Luke 1:26-56

Reflections

Amazing job! You have completed Day 28! A whole month! Way to go!!

If you have been able to be consistent in praying this week—good for you!

If you got off track, make a plan to remedy that and just pick up where you left off.

During your prayer time this week, what has God shown you about Himself?

_____
_____
_____

    About yourself?

_____
_____
_____

In thinking back over the prayers this week...
    Which of the characteristics would you say already describe you? Think of an example of when you demonstrated that trait.

_____
_____
_____

    Did any of the characters or characteristics stand out to you? Why?

_____
_____

Daniel and Ezra demonstrated life-long commitments and authentically lived out their faith. What circumstances in your life make persevering in your faith difficult? What gives you trouble being authentic and living out your faith in your words, your actions, your decisions?

_____

> Take one of those circumstances and write out a prayer asking for God's help, encouragement, and strength. Ask Him to show you how to live your faith and stand up for what you believe in.

_____

Nehemiah and Esther had huge parts to play in the lives of their people. And they rose to the occasion. Nehemiah orchestrated rebuilding the wall around Jerusalem and brought the Law of Moses and true worship back to the people. Esther was instrumental in saving the Jews from genocide. God used them because of who they were and where they were at the right time. Do you sense a call on your life?

Are you in a place now where God can use you for something bigger than you were expecting?
Write a prayer asking God to reveal any plans and purposes He has for your life right now, right where you are.

_____

_____

Job, Habakkuk, and Mary faced unplanned and unexpected situations in their nation and their personal lives. Yet their responses were faith, hope, and joy. Have there been circumstances that have weakened your faith? Stolen your hope? Your joy? List those here.

> In one of those, ask God to build your faith, and return your hope and joy. Let the power and joy of the Lord be your strength. (Nehemiah 8:10)

A Samaritan woman came to get water at the well where Jesus was sitting alone. Knowing her painful background, He initiated a conversation with her, revealing He was the Messiah. She believed and immediately ran to tell others in the town. Because of her passionate testimony, many believed.

DAY 29

Woman at the Well—Passionate

John 4:28-29, 39 *Then, leaving her water jar, the woman went back to the town and said to the people, "Come, see a man who told me everything I ever did. Could this be the Messiah?" Many of the Samaritans from that town believed in him because of the woman's testimony, "He told me everything I ever did."*

Heavenly Father, we have Your Good News. You came to earth and lived a sin-free life. You laid down that life on the cross, suffering and shedding Your blood to pay the price for our sin. Everyone's sin. All of it. And then You rose from the dead leaving behind an empty grave. This is a Gospel worth sharing! And yet there are times when I shrink back from being vocal about my faith.

The Woman at the Well is such a great example of sharing personal testimony. And so easy to follow. I don't need to present spiritual laws or make convincing arguments about theological issues. I can simply share with others, how You have impacted my life. How I see You at work, using my circumstances to bless me, to teach me, to discipline me.

When I understand how You lead me and protect me, I can tell others. I can give comfort and encouragement with the same comfort and encouragement You have given me, and that is all testimony. I don't have to stand up and teach, making speeches or delivering persuasive sermons.

It is the Holy Spirit who calls and saves. I don't do the convincing. But I *am* called to tell what You are doing in my own life. Help me recognize opportunities I have to talk about that. Don't let me be ashamed or embarrassed to speak up. Show me what to say and how to share about my relationship with You. Simply, openly, enthusiastically.

Father, strengthen my character to be like the Woman at the Well: Passionate about sharing You. Amen

Read more about the Woman at the Well: John 4: 4-42

The Royal Official's son was at home in Capernaum close to death. When he heard Jesus was in Cana, he made the trip to beg Jesus to come and heal his son. Jesus simply said, "Go, your son will live," and the Official believed and departed. His faith was rewarded when he received confirmation from his servants while on his way back home. The fever had left his son at the exact time Jesus spoke the words.

DAY 30

The Royal Official—Believing Faith

John 4:49-50, *The royal official said, "Sir, come down before my child dies."*
"Go," Jesus replied, "your son will live."
The man took Jesus at his word and departed.

Heavenly Father, I want this kind of faith to believe even when there is no immediate proof of what You say. This man trusted You completely, enough to simply turn and leave at Your word.

Help me seek You out when I have a need. Forgive me when I come to You last after trying to handle things on my own. I grew up hearing "The Lord helps those who help themselves." It was many years later that I discovered this is not even in the Bible. And certainly does not reflect what You want.

I love the line in the hymn *A Mighty Fortress is our God* that starts the second verse: "Did we in our own strength confide, our striving would be losing." Help me recognize when I need to come to You with my problems, and cease striving on my own.

Often I come to You in a hurry and rattle off my prayer list of thanks and wants. I believe this man's need was so great, that he stood, captive in Your presence, looking intensely into Your eyes. So that when You spoke, there was a deep connection. Father, let me make time in my prayer life, to linger with You. To truly see Your face and look into Your eyes.

That way, when I hear Your voice answering me, I will know that You have heard me, and are answering me, out of Your sovereign power and desire to help. And I can walk away, confident, trusting, believing, without a doubt, that You will do what You say.

Father, strengthen my character to be like the Royal Official: Believing Faith in You. Amen

Read more about the Royal Official: John 4:43-54

The poor widow's offering was two tiny copper coins, amounting to only a few cents. Others put in large amounts, but Jesus saw her heart and recognized that she was offering all she had, and honored her above the others.

DAY 31

Poor Widow—Generous

Mark 12: 43-44, *Calling his disciples to him, Jesus said, "Truly I tell you, this poor widow has put more into the treasury than all the others. They all gave out of their wealth; but she, out of her poverty, put in everything—all she had to live on."*

Heavenly Father, forgive me when I think too much of what I have and am stingy with what You have given me. You love a cheerful giver, so let me give happily of my time, my talent and my treasure for Your purposes and Your glory. Whether it's at the offering plate or through ministry or missions, or some other godly cause, let me hear Your voice showing me how to spend the money, the energy, and the time You have blessed me with on worthy efforts.

Help me set aside time this week to look at where my money goes. And pray about places I could save or spend differently in order to give to Your kingdom. Not just the leftovers from my monthly spending, but show me how to give to You first, out of the abundance of what You have given me.

Let me take a critical look at my daily, weekly and monthly schedule and see where my time goes. Empower me to stop if there are things I waste time on. And to have discipline if there are things I should invest more time in, like relationships, or quality time with You in prayer or reading Your Word, or in some purpose You have for me.

Teach me to be a better steward of the things You've given me, or to embrace opportunities to join in ministries or missions You've made me aware of. Show me if I am valuing my health, my energy, my attention, and using it in a way that brings You honor.

And Father, forgive me when I think too little of what I have to offer. Remind me that You can do amazingly and abundantly more than I can imagine with even a little, when it is offered in faith. Let my pocketbook and my calendar reflect that I trust You with all I have, and let my generosity show it.

Father, strengthen my character to be like this widow: Generous. Amen

Read more about the Widow: Mark 12:41-44; Luke 21:1-4

These four men were aware of their paralyzed friend's needs and when they knew the solution, let nothing, not even a roof, stop them from helping him. Their loyalty carried their friend all the way to Jesus, and when the way was blocked, they climbed up on the roof and created a hole in the roof to lower their friend for Jesus' healing.

DAY 32

Paralyzed Man's friends—Committed

Luke 5:18-19, *Some men came carrying a paralyzed man on a mat and tried to take him into the house to lay him before Jesus. When they could not find a way to do this because of the crowd, they went up on the roof and lowered him on his mat through the tiles into the middle of the crowd, right in front of Jesus.*

Heavenly Father, I want to be like these friends of the paralyzed man. Encourage me to make the time to be aware when my friends have needs. That may mean making time in my schedule to spend with them, and really listen. Help me speak words of kindness, comfort, encouragement, guidance, love. Let me spend my time on my friends, keeping their confidences. sharing in their sorrows as well as joys.

Let me not only speak it, but demonstrate friendship by my actions. Empower me to help when I can support or make a difference, spending my energy and resources on the people who are important in my life. Even if it means going against what might typically be expected by acting extravagantly or helping in unique, "out of the box" ways that You show me.

Father, thank You for the precious friends You have brought into my life. For the ways they enrich my life with their presence and all they ways they help and support me. Let them know they can count on me. Prompt me to pray for them, especially during times of hardship and challenge. And reveal how I can show my appreciation for all they mean to me.

Father, strengthen my character to be like the Paralyzed Man's friends: Committed to act when needed. Amen

Read more about these friends: Mark 2:1-5; Luke 5:17-26

This woman had had a bleeding issue for twelve years and had spent all she had on failed treatments. She believed that if she could only touch the hem of Jesus' garment, she would be healed. In her conviction, she dared approach Jesus, a man, and a Rabbi who she was socially forbidden to approach. And her bleeding issue made her unclean, compounding the inappropriateness to her daring act. But by doing so she received complete healing.

DAY 33

Bleeding Woman—Daring

Luke 8:44, *She came up behind him and touched the edge of his cloak, and immediately her bleeding stopped.*

Heavenly Father, this woman had amazing faith! It was so strong she dared to act. Her conviction drove her to risk reprisal, in order to receive Your miraculous, complete healing.

What would I dare, what would I do, to receive an answer to prayer…even a miracle? Do I let the circumstances **around me** determine how much I am willing to trust my faith?

It's easy for me to believe You healed people in the Bible. And when people tell me how You've acted in their lives, I believe that too. But I sometimes feel so unworthy that I doubt You will answer my prayers or act in my life. My faith doesn't dare much. Father, diminish my fear and grow my faith!

I want to act on my faith like this woman. I want to be bold and blessed! My faith is not dependent on me or how the circumstances look from an earthly perspective. My faith is in the One who is worthy!

Help me be bold and daring. Remind me to look to You and call on You first. You have promised to never leave me. Recall to my mind all the times You have been faithful to me in the past. Do not let me forget the ways You have walked beside me through hard times, answered my prayers in unique and amazing ways, even worked miraculously on my behalf. Thank You for being the Author and Perfecter of my faith.

Father, strengthen my character to be like the Bleeding Woman: Daring. Amen

Read more about the Bleeding Woman: Mark 5:21-34; Luke 8:40-48

In Jesus' parable, this was an ordinary man from Samaria (a people looked down on by the Jews). At his own expense, he took pity on and cared for a total stranger who had been beaten and robbed. And went the extra mile when a Priest and Levite had passed him by, not helping at all. This Samaritan personifies a "neighbor" in the Good Samaritan teaching.

DAY 34

Good Samaritan—Caring

Luke 10:33-34, *But a Samaritan, as he traveled, came where the man was; and when he saw him, he took pity on him. He went to him and bandaged his wounds, pouring on oil and wine. Then he put the man on his own donkey, brought him to an inn and took care of him.*

Heavenly Father, help me be like Jesus' example of the Good Samaritan. Give me Your perspective to see that everything I have is a blessing from You. And that I am to share that blessing…with everyone. Not just people who look or think like me.

You have commanded us to love our neighbor as ourselves. Open my eyes to see who is hurting right where I am—where You have put me. Help me look beyond our differences and see when there are people hurting, grieving or in need. And give me Your heart to help them however I can.

This story Jesus told goes beyond just being caring. It speaks to a level of spiritual hypocrisy and political bigotry of the men who passed by. The Samaritan was able to look past the social discrimination that the Priest and Levite demonstrated, to help the wounded man.

Remove greed, selfishness, discrimination and hypocrisy from me. And let me emerge from this crisis of disunity in my country, a more loving, caring person who brings honor to Your name.

Father, strengthen my character to be like Jesus' story character, the Good Samaritan: Caring and willing to help others. Amen

Read more about The Good Samaritan: Luke 10:25-37

Lepers were made ceremonially unclean by their disease, and as such, were made to live outside towns or communities and were forbidden from touching anyone. Many might gather to live together away from their families and scavenge for food. Ten lepers saw Jesus approaching a village and shouted out for healing. When Jesus healed them, only one returned to thank Jesus for the miraculous healing.

DAY 35

The One Leper—Thankful

Luke 17:15-19, *One of them, when he saw he was healed, came back, praising God in a loud voice. He threw himself at Jesus' feet and thanked him—and he was a Samaritan. Jesus asked, "Were not all ten cleansed? Where are the other nine? Has no one returned to give praise to God except this foreigner?" Then he said to him, "Rise and go; your faith has made you well."*

Heavenly Father, I don't know why only one leper returned to thank You. But it does speak to my heart of how often I too, forget to thank You. I take for granted so many things until I am reminded like this. Or until I see someone who is worse off than I or has bigger problems. Or until I lose something, and realize I wasn't really grateful while I had it.

Thank You for the good times I've experienced and the blessings I've received from You. I want to begin every day with thanks and praise to You for life, for breath, for energy to rise, for clothes to wear, clean water to drink, food to eat, clear thinking to reason with, a home to live in, transportation, education, work, church, purpose, support and encouragement.

I am grateful for the Bible, the Holy Spirit, the direction and protection I get from You. Thankful for Your faithfulness to Your promises for my life here on earth and for my eternal salvation and future with You. Thank You for loved ones in my life, family and friends who care, for faith, hope, and love. Help me express my gratitude and thank You in word, in song, in praise, in the way I treat others, for such blessings in my life!

And I thank You for the trials. For growing my faith through them and giving me the patient endurance, I need to learn and grow from, gain Your perspective on, and outlast the trials.

> Thank You for the bitter things
> They've been a friend to grace,
> They've driven me from paths of ease
> To storm the secret place.
> —Florence White Willett

Father, strengthen my character to be like the One Leper: Thankful. Amen

Read more about the One Leper: Luke 17:11-19

Reflections

You're almost there! Amazing job!! We are so proud of you!

If you have been able to be consistent in praying this week—good for you!

If you got off track, make a plan to remedy that and just pick up where you left off. You can do it!

During your prayer time this week, what has God shown you about Himself?

_____

About yourself?

_____

In thinking back over the prayers this week...
Which of the characteristics would you say already describe you? Think of an example of when you demonstrated that trait.

_____

Did any of the characters or characteristics stand out to you? Why?

_____

Like the Woman at the Well, what opportunities have you had this week to share your faith with other people? Just simply talk about how God has impacted your life? Describe those times and whether you shared or not.

_____

What keeps you from sharing more often?

_____

Ask God to fan the flame of your passion to share your faith.

_____

Thinking of the Royal Official and the Bleeding Woman - how strong is your faith? If God simply told you something would happen, would you count on it? Would you do something daring, radical, to demonstrate your belief?

> Our actions speak louder than our words. The Paralyzed Man's Friends acted radically to receive the healing they believed Jesus would give. What do your actions say about your faith?

_____

Our faith can grow when we recall the times God has been faithful to us in the past. And when we see Him being faithful to others. List some times God has shown up for you, or for another.

_____

_____

_____

The Poor Widow and the Good Samaritan are examples of being generous with our blessings—money, time, energy. And being willing to go out of our way or do without so someone else can be blessed. Write about when you made a sacrifice so others could be blessed.

> If an opportunity comes up, ask God to show you how to be a cheerful giver and a caring neighbor.

In all things, give thanks! (1 Thessalonians 5:16) Jot a prayer of thanks here for ways you've seen God at work in your life this week. If you're not sure what those are, spend a few minutes thinking back through the last seven days and ask God to open your eyes to what He's done for you.

> There may not be a miraculous healing like the Leper this week, but every breath we take is a gift: as is food, clothing, housing, health, transportation, friends, family, work, ministry, purpose, freedom...that might help get you started.

The blind beggar outside Jericho knew who Jesus was and called out for His mercy as He was passing by. Even though others tried to shut him up the blind man continued to call out and ask for his sight. Jesus stopped and healed him instantly, miraculously, causing all to give praise to God.

DAY 36

The Blind Beggar—Persistent

Luke 18:39, *Those who led the way rebuked him and told him to be quiet, but he shouted all the more, "Son of David, have mercy on me!"*

Heavenly Father, let me learn from this blind beggar. When I have a need, help me see it for what it is, not hide it or deny it. And let me come straight to You; confident that You have the desire and the power to help.

There are so many things I am already trusting You for...I may not be blind but sometimes I don't even know what I need. Open my eyes so I know what to even ask You for in my relationships, my work, my physical, emotional, financial, mental, social and spiritual life. Help me see where I am just getting by and how I can improve by seeking Your direction, Your purpose for my life.

Remind me to be persistent like the blind beggar was. If others rebuke me or try and stop me from seeking You in my circumstances, do not let me be dissuaded by those influences. The world rebukes us by saying we ought to be able to help ourselves, do things on our own. Even our own inner voices can be critical when we ask for help.

Vulnerability is not valued. And our society certainly does not honor weakness, or even like to admit it or let it show. And yet it's often the spaces or gaps that our weaknesses create, that allow You to work.

I know You have what I need: answers - direction - wisdom - healing - miracles! Don't let me give up before I hear from You. Help me to resist being "shushed" by those around me, well-meaning or not, when I know the request is inspired by You.

Father, strengthen my character to be like the Blind Beggar: Persistent in asking when I have a need. Amen

Read more about the Blind Beggar: Mark 10:46-52; Luke 18:35-42

Zacchaeus was a wealthy tax-collector; considered a traitor by the Jews for overtaxing his own people. But he had a curiosity and hunger to know about Jesus. Jesus went out of his way and changed Zacchaeus' life forever. Zacchaeus became charitable and willing to acknowledge and right his wrongs.

DAY 37

Zacchaeus—Curious

Luke 19:3-4, *He wanted to see who Jesus was, but because he was short he could not see over the crowd. So he ran ahead and climbed a sycamore-fig tree to see him.*

Heavenly Father, give me a curiosity, a hunger to know You better. Let me be willing to do whatever I need to do to see and hear from You personally. Even if it means doing something that makes me look silly to others—like climbing a tree as Zacchaeus did!

I want to be enthusiastic about my faith in You and welcome You gladly into my home.

- It may mean passing up social opportunities in order to attend church or a Bible study group.
- It may mean giving my time and money to help build Your kingdom here rather than my earthly estate.
- It may mean having a serious conversation with a friend about spiritual issues instead of just hanging out or watching the game.
- It may mean saying a prayer of thanks over my food in a crowded restaurant, when no one else is.

Simply being with Jesus convicted Zacchaeus' heart to confess his sin and make retribution. Father, remind me to set aside time to hear from You. Show me how to grow in my spiritual life and open my spiritual eyes and ears to hear and respond with understanding and obedience. Show me where I need to right any wrongs I've done. Let being in Your presence affect me deeply, and change me.

Father, strengthen my character to be like Zacchaeus: Curious to know more of You. Amen

Read more about Zacchaeus: Luke 19:1-10

The Apostle Paul was a Roman citizen by birth, and a Jewish Pharisee who persecuted Christians until a miraculously revealing encounter with Jesus. At that point he became a Christian missionary, traveling and performing miracles. He wrote at least seven books of the New Testament; teaching, encouraging and building up Christians in their faith. He did this while being in prison, and was eventually martyred for his faith.

DAY 38

Paul—Encourager

Philippians 3:13-14, *"Forgetting what is behind and straining toward what is ahead, I press on toward the goal to win the prize for which God has called me heavenward in Christ Jesus."*

Heavenly Father, let my life be an encouragement to others, like Paul. Whether by telling others about You and how to be saved, or encouraging those who already believe. Give me a heart for the lost who are living their life without You. And show me how to help those who are hurting or doubting their faith.

Show me how to embrace the opportunities You give me to tell others about You through the circumstances of my life and the people I meet along the way. Let me influence others by spreading Your Gospel.

Make me bold to share the impact You've had on my own life: how You have answered prayers, delivered me from dangerous circumstances, directed my decisions, healed me, and comforted me in hardship.

Strengthen me to talk about how You have encouraged me in my faith over and over again by working in my job, in my relationships, my challenges and my joys. Let me write, like Paul did to others who are in hard times, speaking words of reassurance and inspiration to help them. Spur me on to send cards or letters, emails or texts; to make phone calls and connect with others to provide help and support.

And remind me to pray for those You bring to me in my life: my spouse and children and their spouses and children, my friends, my pastor and church, those I work with, as well as those You make me aware of and bring to mind in my own country and around the world who are living in hardship: victims of disaster, injustice or persecution.

Father, strengthen my character to be like Paul: an amazing Encourager. Amen

Read more about Paul: the Book of Acts, Galatians, Ephesians, Philippians

I believe as we have walked through the Bible,
God may have brought another character to your mind.
Maybe someone we haven't talked or prayed about.
Or maybe you have had a character in mind since we
started, and they haven't been listed.

Picture that character now, or ask God to bring someone to mind. Look up the scripture that tells about them. Choose a characteristic from them that you want to imitate. Put their name or their character trait into the blanks in the prayer.

DAY 39

You Choose

2 Timothy 3:16 -17, *All Scripture is God-breathed and is useful for teaching, rebuking, correcting and training in righteousness, so that the servant of God may be thoroughly equipped for every good work.*

Heavenly Father, thank You for drawing my mind to _____. I appreciate the character trait of _____ displayed by their actions or their life. In this way I want to be more like them.

I may not face what they faced, or have a similar outcome in my life, but I want my character to reflect this godly characteristic.

Father, open my eyes to ways I can learn _____. Help me change whatever I need to change. Help me turn away from ungodly ways and see from Your perspective how this quality of _____ will help me.

Thank You for opening my eyes and giving me understanding to see how to become more godly—in my thoughts, my words, my actions, my relationships, and how I make decisions. Show me the small steps I need to make; steps that will lead toward the changes You and I want to see in me.

Father, strengthen my character to be like _____: clearly displaying _____ for Your glory. Amen

DAY 40

Aaronic Blessing

Heavenly Father, as Aaron, the High Priest, gave this blessing over the people of Israel every year, I pray it now over myself as I finish this amazing prayer journey. I pray this blessing as a reassuring reminder, not only of Your amazing and powerful presence and protection for me, but of Your desire and ability to fulfill the purpose You created me for.

Defining the six Hebrew verbs adds a deeper understanding of the blessing's meaning. These expanded definitions of the six Hebrew verbs in this blessing come from Bill Bullock, The Rabbi's Son. Find him on www.biblicallifestylecenter.org

May You, Lord God, the Holy One, infuse me with unlimited potential and power and release me from any restrictions or limitations that would prevent me from reaching the fullness of my potential to participate in my divine purpose which You have given me.

May You zealously cherish and treasure me, diligently defending and keeping watch over me to protect and save me.

May the light of Your innermost being and essence illuminate me physiologically and spiritually, impacting my body, mind, soul and spirit with Your warming, healing, soothing, restorative, empowering and constantly renewing energy.

May You, the Holy One, give me what I really need, not because I've earned it, or out of pity, benevolence, or even generosity, but because You have promised, as the stronger covenant partner, to strengthen me and enable me to reach my potential and enjoy the covenant You entered into with me, when I accepted You as Savior.

As You were face to face with the High Priest in the Holy of Holies, may You be present with me so I can experience true spiritual reality.

And may You place in and establish in me, wholeness, wellness, purposeful living in joy, with abundant provision, harmony, safety, security summed up in the Hebrew word "Shalom" translated as "peace."

The "Priestly Blessing"

Y'varechecha Adonai
[May the Holy One bless you]

v'yish'merecha
[and zealously cherish and keep watch over you]

Ya'er Adonai panav elecha
[May the Holy One's Face shine upon you]

v'chuneka
[and shower you with grace]

Yisa Adonai panav elecha
[May the Holy One lift up His countenance upon you]

v'yasem lecha shalom
[and may He give you wholeness, wellness, security, abundant provision, and peace].

[Numbers 6:24-26]

Reflections

CONGRATULATIONS!! You made it!!
You finished the work you started! You did it! The whole 40 days!
We are so proud of you!!
How does it feel?

In thinking back over the prayers this week...
> Which of the characteristics would you say already describe you? Think of an example of when you demonstrated that trait.

___

> Did any of the characters or characteristics stand out to you? Why?

___

Like the Blind Beggar, do you have a need to bring to God? Write what it is, and be prepared to be persistent in praying about it. When I was young I heard the acronym PUSH—Pray Until Something Happens. It may be that God will grant what you ask for. Or the "something" that happens may be that God answers with a "No" or a "Wait."

Is there something about God that makes you curious? Write what that is and how willing you are to set aside time to hear from Him, like Zacchaeus did. Seek Him and let Him change you.

___

To share God's power in your life to encourage others, you need to recognize God's power in your life. Spend some time recalling how God has worked in your life in the past. Write those down. Maybe make a timeline on a sheet of paper and fill in points where you felt close to God, or saw where your faith had an impact on your path.

___

Can you think of 3 people you could share some of those with? Ask God to open your eyes to opportunities to share how He has impacted your life to encourage or inspire others.

_____

_____

During your 40 day prayer journey, has God shown you anything new about Himself?

_____

      How will you apply that to your life?

      _____

Has God shown you anything new about yourself? Taught you anything about your character?

_____

      Ask God to continue to show you characters in the Bible who inspire you to grow in your character.

Have a time of Thanksgiving! Thank about the past 40 days or this past year and give God thanks in prayer, or jot a note here:
      For the ways you've seen Him at work in your life…

      For the things you have, or don't have…

      For the things He's allowed into your life, and those things He's protected you from…

      For the blessing of prayer and the answers to prayers…

Do you feel encouraged to do another 40 Day Prayer Journey?

Select one of our books for powerful, prewritten prayers to pray for someone's salvation or blessing. Or ask God to show you the next topic to pray about that would benefit from your prayerful attention for the next 40 day journey!

AFTERWARDS
Thank You After 40 Days

Heavenly Father, thank You for this journey of praying intentionally and consistently for these 40 days. Thank You for Your promise to hear me when I call to You. And to answer my prayers. I believe Your Word will not return void, and as I have prayed Your Word and asked for You to teach me, I am trusting that it will continue to bear fruit long after these 40 days have passed.

I pray that through these prayers Your power will be released in my life to continue my character and spiritual growth. Keep my eyes and ears open to examples in scripture I can learn from. Whether its everyday people or the Lord Jesus Christ, show me how their character traits are something I should either imitate or avoid.

Speak to me from the parables to show me the values I need to follow in order to have godly character. Call my attention to issues or actions in the Bible that I can apply to my own circumstances.

Teach me from metaphors that illustrate how I should behave: like being a sheep who knows their Shepherd's voice, or shining like a lamp on a stand, or becoming like a tree planted by the water.

Do not let me forget the things I've learned about You, about prayer and about myself and my character during these 40 days. I continue to pray that You will make Your presence known and Your blessings felt in my life. That I will sense You at work, in large ways and in small ones.

And as opportunities arise to make these character changes, steer me in the right direction and give me victory in making godly choices. And over time, let these choices become habit and part of my character.

I am continually grateful that I can pray for Your will and Your purpose in my life. May I never ever forget that I am Your child. And that You are with me always. May that remembrance be a powerful deterrent and an awesome reassurance.

Thank You for hearing and answering my prayers—in ways that are above and beyond what I could ever ask for or even imagine. Thank You for strengthening me on my journey. Amen

APPENDICES

APPENDIX A

Confession and Repentance

Let God speak to you now and show you any sin you need to confess. Psalm 66:18 tells us if we cherish sin in our hearts, God won't listen to our prayers. Tell God you are willing to turn away from those things (which is repentance) and ask for His forgiveness.

1 John 1:9-10 tells us "If we confess our sins, He is faithful and righteous to forgive us our sins and to cleanse us from all unrighteousness. If we claim we have not sinned, we make Him a liar, and His word is not in us."

Ask God if there are sins of:

THOUGHT—impure, selfish, angry, fearful, jealous
ATTITUDE—prideful, judgmental, argumentative, lukewarm toward God
SPEECH—crude, inappropriate, grumbling, divisive, lies, half-truths
RELATIONSHIP—wrong or improper, physically or emotionally

    Do you need to forgive someone? Do you need to ask for forgiveness?

    As a husband: are you providing spiritual leadership, guiding and nurturing your wife?

    As a wife: are you honoring and respecting your husband?

    As parents: are you modeling godly behavior and attitudes and teaching your children in love?

    As children or teens: are you respectful and obedient?

COMMISSION—things that you have done, actions you have taken

    Have you done something you know is wrong?

    Do you guard your eyes?

    Have you exposed yourself to the occult?

    Do you have habits that are harmful to your body - mind - spirit?

OMISSION—things you have failed to do

    Has God prompted you to do something you haven't done?

    Have you failed to do good when you could have?

SELF-RULE—rebellion, going your own way

    Are you following God or going your own way?

    Are you avoiding something He's told you to do?

    Or are you still doing something He's told you not to?

APPENDIX B

Spiritual Armor for Battle

Ephesians 6:10-18 *Finally, be strong in the Lord and in his mighty power. Put on the full armor of God, so that you can take your stand against the devil's schemes. For our struggle is not against flesh and blood, but against the rulers, against the authorities, against the powers of this dark world and against the spiritual forces of evil in the heavenly realms. Therefore put on the full armor of God, so that when the day of evil comes, you may be able to stand your ground, and after you have done everything, to stand. Stand firm then, with the belt of truth buckled around your waist, with the breastplate of righteousness in place, and with your feet fitted with the readiness that comes from the gospel of peace. In addition to all this, take up the shield of faith, with which you can extinguish all the flaming arrows of the evil one. Take the helmet of salvation and the sword of the Spirit, which is the word of God.*

And pray in the Spirit on all occasions with all kinds of prayers and requests. With this in mind, be alert and always keep on praying for all the Lord's people.

We dress ourselves in the armor that Paul describes here. He wrote his letter to the Ephesians while he was in Rome, under house arrest, guarded by Roman soldiers. Every day, he saw men dressed in armor, bearing the insignia of their authority. The Holy Spirit must have inspired his analogy of a Christian "soldier."

> **Praying on the armor can be as simple as listing each piece and stating that you are putting it on and wearing it.**

When we are praying for someone, or even ourselves, the devil doesn't like it. And even with his limited power here on earth, we can find ourselves under attack in ways that can lead us to feel discouraged, defeated, even want to give up.

But we rely on the fact that God's armor is the very best!

The **Belt of Truth** is a wide, tight band around the waist that holds pieces of the armor on as well as the sword. When we are wearing truth we can more easily recognize the lies the devil would tempt us to believe. We will not be mesmerized by half-truths or deceptions.

The **Breastplate of Righteousness** protects our heart and vital organs, a kind of forerunner of the bulletproof vest. It stops and deflects stabs and projectiles, keeping our heart and spirit from evil deceptions. Our righteousness comes from Jesus Christ. His blood paid the price for our sin and we gain the righteousness of the perfect life He lived. In that righteousness the devil cannot hold anything against us.

The **Shoes of the Gospel of Peace** will help us walk in the Spirit. Putting on shoes is a sign of readiness and preparedness. With these we are ready to carry the Good News of salvation and peace into our relationships and whatever challenges we face. With our feet protected like this we will have traction even when we feel unsteady, and will be able to stand firm.

The **Shield of Faith** is not some puny little garbage can lid with a handle, but a head to toe protection, repelling the enemy's offensive weapons. When the shield was anointed with oil it would reflect the glare of the sun and blind the enemy. This shield covered a soldier from top to bottom, side to side and can join with others to form a wall of protection that will fend off an attacker while advancing in the field of battle.

Our faith in God protects us when the world or others tells us things are hopeless or cannot work out because we have the One True God who is all-knowing and all-powerful. We trust in His love for us and know that He has a plan for us, to give us hope and a future with Him in eternity. Every time He keeps a promise, or delivers us from some trouble, or stands with us in hardship, it builds or faith - strengthens our shields! And when we stand beside other believers in their faith, we are protected even more!

The **Helmet of Salvation** protects our head and identifies who we fight for. This helmet also protects our minds and helps guard our thoughts. The enemy would want to fill our minds with thoughts of doubt, fear and insecurity. But when thoughts and emotional responses are stirred up, we can hold them up to the light of truth: scripture. God's Word is the truth that will combat all that would discourage us.

And the **Sword of the Spirit** is God's Word, and strikes at the lies the devil would use to try and defeat us. We can use it to refute any lies the devil tries to get us to believe. We can pray it as part of our prayers. We can speak it out loud as an attack on the enemy. There is power in the Word of God.

Here is a sample prayer:

Heavenly Father, I come before you with thanks for the armor that You give me, which is the best. With the belt of truth fastened around my waist, I say that I will not believe the lies the devil would try to use to confuse me. Give me clarity and understanding. Help me see past what the world and others would tell me, to what you want to say to me.

I wear the helmet of salvation to guard my mind, and I take every thought captive to You. The breastplate of righteousness I place over my chest to protect my heart.

I wear the shoes of peace to say that I am ready to hear from You and to obey what You tell me to do and follow where You lead.

I take up my shield to repel all the arguments the evil one would send against me. And I take up the sword, the Word of God, as a weapon to help me stand firm against the devil's schemes.

Thank you for hearing my prayer. Amen.

APPENDIX C
How you tune in to God's voice

I believe God is speaking to us, or sending out His signal, all the time, through His Word, His Son, His Creation, and our circumstances, among other ways. His is a constant, uninterruptible, full-strength signal. But we need to tune in to hear it.

God has given us, built into us, a receiver to hear Him. It's our spirit. We are all made up of body, mind and spirit. As a believer, we also have the Holy Spirit within us who helps us hear Him even better. And the Holy Spirit helps us understand what we hear.

His is a perfect "wireless" connection that is never out of service, out of range, broken, interrupted by weather conditions, satellite position, or earthly circumstances. But here are three reasons we may not be "tuned in."

1 We don't know God's frequencies?

> Prayer—Scripture—Nature—Circumstances—
> Dreams—Pain—Sermons—Bible Study—
> People—Podcasts—Christian books—Revelations

Ask yourself—Are you tuning in to and exposing yourself to the sources God is broadcasting on?

> Make time for those opportunities regularly in your day, your week. Ask God to speak to you in ways you will notice and understand. You might try a "Tune In Exercise" in the next section of the Appendix.

2 Like your physical ears, we can't hear clearly if the noise level around us is drowning out what God is saying. And we have inner voices we often focus on that keep us from hearing what God has to say.

Ask yourself—Are you paying more attention to what you hear in the world and within yourself?

Invite the Holy Spirit to silence all ungodly sources and distractions. Ask that confusion, preconceived ideas, biases, and misconceptions be sent away. And ask the Holy Spirit to reveal truth, clarify meaning, and show application to your life.

3 You have an ear infection. Spiritually, sin can block our ability to communicate effectively with God.

Ask yourself—Have you cleaned out your spiritual ears lately?

Be willing to confess your sin to God and turn from it. He will forgive you and that will re-establish your communication.

For more information, see Confession and Repentance in Appendix A.

APPENDIX D
Tune In Exercise for Hearing God

God speaks in so many different ways, I can't list them all. He is so creative and you are unique. Here are 4 exercises you can try that have worked for others.

Begin by asking God to speak to you in a way that you will recognize and understand. He WILL answer your prayer. Although it can happen, you may not hear an audible, physical voice.

1—Set aside a time to get alone and just be still. Arrange for no interruptions. Turn off your cell phone or anything else that might distract you. For some people it helps to be outdoors without the distractions of the house or apartment. For others, a quiet room works.

Start a conversation with God. You can speak out loud, or with your inner voice, He can hear you. Begin by thanking God - for who He is, for something He's done in your life or in the world. Or begin with a question you have, or share with Him something that's weighing on your heart or concerning you.

Then quiet yourself and listen. Eyes open are ok unless that distracts you. Eyes closed works too. Ask the Holy Spirit to help you sense what God is saying. He may speak to you in words of comfort, or love, instruction or change your perspective. He may place a picture or vision in your mind. He may sing you a song or direct you to scripture.

Write down what you hear. Then check it against scripture in the Hearing God Worksheet in the Appendix.

2—Plan uninterrupted time without others nearby to observe what is around you.

If you can go outside, are there birds, trees, flowers, clouds, mountains, water, some piece of God's creation that might have a message for you? Do you see something that shows you something about yourself, or about God? Do you see something that reflects some inner truth?

If inside, look out a window, or at art, or the colors or items around you and check any memories or feelings they evoke. Do you need a fresh look at an area of your life? Do you need help dealing with emotions that may have surfaced?

3—Get alone in a comfortable place where you can read or listen. Open your Bible or listen to scripture being read aloud. If you've been reading regularly, start where you left off. If not you might consider looking at the One Year Bible website and choose the scripture selection for that day. God may direct you to a place to begin. If this is new to you, start with the book of John. Or Joshua. Or 1 John.

Start reading and read until you hear something that resonates with something you are going through. It may be a message of instruction, or encouragement, or a revelation about yourself or God. A verse may stand out with a new significance or a better understanding than it has had before. Or it may shine a light that gives you a new perspective.

Ask what this means. And what it means to you. Is there something you need to change—to do, or stop doing with this new understanding? Is there a warning you need to heed? An example for you to follow? Is God showing you something about Himself? About yourself in these verses?

4—Freestyle—Talk to God Wherever you are, whenever—day or night, whatever the circumstances. You can say anything to Him. Whisper your fears, yell your frustrations, rage against your circumstances. He can take it all. Pour out your heart about what you are facing. Ask for His perspective. Or for clarification on an issue.

Are you experiencing blessing? Confusion? Pain? What in your circumstances is speaking the loudest? Ask God to show you where He is in that circumstance and ask Him for wisdom to cope with it. What you can learn from it. How can you share the blessing? What can you learn from your pain? Who can you connect with because of your blessing, confusion or pain?

Then pause to hear His answer. Do you need a change of attitude? A course correction? Do you hear a word of encouragement? Direction? Or feel a sense of comfort? Can you comfort, direct or encourage someone else with what you hear?

APPENDIX E
Hearing from God

Proverbs 8:32-5 *"Now then, my children, listen to me;*
blessed are those who keep my ways.
Listen to my instruction and be wise;
do not disregard it.
Blessed are those who listen to me,
watching daily at my doors,
waiting at my doorway.
For those who find me find life
and receive favor from the Lord.

But how do I know if what I hear is from God or some other voice??
When you believe you've heard from God You, write it down and put it to the test.
Ask these three questions to see if you heard it from God or some other source:

1—Does what I hear agree with the Bible?

The answer must be "yes." God will never tell you anything that contradicts what He has already said in His Word. So, spend time in and be familiar with the Bible.

If you need help, a Christian friend or pastor can help you find scripture dealing with your topic. If there is nothing, or you are unsure, ask God to reveal the truth to you.

One role of the Holy Spirit who dwells in every believer is to teach us, guiding us in truth. In John 14:26, Jesus tells us the Holy Spirit will teach us all things. And in John 16:13 tells us the Holy Spirit will guide us into all truth.

2—Will the result, or the fruit of the act be the fruit of the Spirit?

This answer should also be "yes." The result of what you hear should lead to and produce the fruit of the Spirit in your life and those around you.

Galatians 5:19-23 outlines the fruit of the Spirit as: love, joy, peace, patience, kindness, goodness, faithfulness, gentleness, and self-control.

Verses 19-21 tell us the acts of the flesh are immorality, impurity, debauchery, idolatry, witchcraft, hatred, discord, jealousy, rage, selfish ambition, dissension, envy, and the like.

So if you act on what you think God is telling you, what will happen? Look at the expected result, or the "fruit," to see where it leads.

3 – Will it benefit my relationship with God?

Again, **this answer should be "yes."** Everything you do will benefit or weaken your relationship with God.

Micah 6:8 *And what does the LORD require of you? To act justly and to love mercy and to walk humbly with your God.*

Most of the time, the Holy Spirit will tell you if what you are doing is pulling you away from God. You will probably be able to sense that you are either drawing closer to God or pulling away if you were to follow through on what you think you hear Him telling you.

It might help to ask another Christian friend, pastor or counselor. Or even pose the question: What Would Jesus do?

If you hit a "no" stop right there! What you heard is **NOT from God.** If it
> **does NOT agree with the Bible**, or
>
> **does NOT produce the Fruit of the Spirit**, or
>
> **does NOT benefit your relationship with God**,
>
> then it is NOT from God.

So what do you do ?

If you got a NO -

Pray for strength to say "no" to that and keep seeking God's wisdom.

James 1:5 says *"If any of you lacks wisdom, you should ask God, who gives generously to all without finding fault, and it will be given to you."* So ask again for God's input.

If you got 3 YES -

Pray for the strength and courage to follow through on what God has shown you.

Paul encourages us that we can do all things through Christ who strengthens us. Philippians 4:13

If confusion still exists, go back and ask God for clarity. And be patient. The answer may be unclear because the timing isn't right. Be willing to wait on God's timing.

Psalm 27:14 *Wait for the LORD; be strong and take heart and wait for the LORD.*

APPENDIX F

Hearing from God Worksheet

Is what I'm hearing from God?

James 1:5 *If any of you lacks wisdom, you should ask God, who gives generously to all without finding fault, and it will be given to you.*

If you hit a "No" stop there. Is it NOT from God.

What is my concern or question
What am I hearing?
What does the Bible say about my concern and what I am hearing?
Does what I am hearing agree with the Bible? ❏Y ❏N
If I act on what I've heard, what will it produce in my life and others?
Is that a Fruit of the Spirit? ❏Y ❏N
If I act on what I've heard, will it benefit my relationship with God? ❏Y ❏N

APPENDIX G

Fasting

Fasting is a spiritual discipline taught in the Bible. Jesus expected His followers to fast and said that God rewards fasting. He gave us some instruction as well:

> *"When you fast, do not look somber like the hypocrites do, for they disfigure their faces to show men they are fasting. I tell you the truth, they have received their reward in full. But when you fast, put oil on your head and wash your face, so that it will not be obvious to men that you are fasting, but only to your Father, who is unseen; and your Father, who sees what is done in secret, will reward you," Matthew 6:16-18*

Often in the Bible, God's people fasted right before a major victory, miracle or answer to prayer. It prepared them to hear and receive from God. Moses fasted before receiving the 10 Commandments (Exodus 34:28); Nehemiah before he undertook a great work for God (Nehemiah 1:4); Esther and her people before she sought the favor of the king to save her people (Esther 4:15-17); early Christians at a time of decision (Acts 13:2-3). And of course Jesus fasted.

HOWEVER, be assured that fasting is:
>> NOT as much about food as it is about focus
>> NOT as much about saying no to the body
>>> as it is about saying yes to the Spirit
>> NOT about doing without, but about looking within

This is something we can do to demonstrate to God the depth of our desire to submit before Him, asking Him to "clear our plate" of anything in us that is not of Him. Also in scripture, when there was holy work to be done, those involved would fast to cleanse themselves spiritually in preparation to be used by God.

Fasting means to reduce or eliminate your intake of food or a behavior for a specific time and purpose. You can use the time you'd normally spend in these activities for reading scripture and prayer. Whenever you think of food, or the activity, use it as a prompt to pray.

Your time in prayer should include all aspects of communication with our Father:

Praise Him for who He is. Read scripture, like Psalm 8, 33, 103 or sing some praise songs.

Repent: Confess your sin, turn from it and be cleansed before Him. Read Psalm 32, 51, or Isaiah 59:1-2

Ask for His blessing on your life, your family, your church, your community, your country, or an issue you've been dealing with

Yield to His response. Pray expecting to hear answers, allowing for time to just listen. Read scripture to see what He has to say to you.

Are you ready to consider a fast? Some types of fasts are:
- Water fast—abstain from all food and juices
- Juice fast—only drink fruit and vegetable juices
- Partial fast—eliminate certain foods or specific meal
- Non-food fast—like watching TV, using social media or the internet, talking, or some other activity you normally spend time on

The length of a fast can vary as well. Please be wise and evaluate your participation with your personal health needs.

Whether you eat or not, this can be a great opportunity to set aside a time to feast on the LORD to show that you are:

willing to be humbled and molded before Him
willing to be cleansed and set apart to do His will
willing to sacrifice personal pleasure for time with Him

"So we fasted and prayed to God about this, and He answered our prayer."
Ezra 8:23

About the Authors

Eric Sprinkle: A former Whitewater Guide and Swift-water Rescue Instructor for the U.S. military, Eric travels the country speaking about the benefits of risk, managing fear, and how to make life more exciting by "living a slightly more dangerous lifestyle." If any of the book's images capture or inspire you? That's Jesus' fault for giving him traits like Risk-Taking, Daring, and being Adventurous. Find more on him at AdventureExperience.net, including Speaker info, free photos, and an action-packed YouTube channel full of waterfalls, cliff faces, and whitewater silliness.

Laura Shaffer: An Army Brat moving almost every year till college, Laura was delighted to discover that wherever she went, God was always there ahead of her. Even though the houses, and friends changed, there was always Sunday School and church where she learned that God was always with her. And she felt it.

Through the years she continued in her awareness of God's presence, especially working in the yard and taking nature walks in beautiful, colorful, Colorado. She writes to encourage people to lean into God and learn from Him in their daily life through nature, scripture, circumstances and prayer.

And now she wants to help you experience God's presence—equipping you to pray more intentionally and consistently, to empower your prayer life, and deepen your relationship with God.

Check out Laura's blog at www.DailyBiblePrayer.wordpress.com for scripture-based examples of her prayers anytime

Additional Thoughts on Praying for Character

Need an Adventure Speaker for your next event or group meet-up?

Need someone to talk about
- Risk and Challenge
- Making your life more Exciting
- Dealing better with Fear

Eric would love to hang out with your group!

He's ready to unpack the question of whether our Lord God calls us to adventure, and even share some fun stories about prayer books too! All with heart pounding stories and gorgeous photos!

Check out AdventureExperience.net today and let's connect for an inspiring, challenging time together!

Additional Thoughts on Praying for Character

LOVE LAURA'S PRAYERS?

Looking for more from your new prayer partner Laura?

You've got it!

Have a look here for daily prayers, inspiring blogs, and more!

Check out her prayer blog—
www.dailyBibleprayer.wordpress.com

For her devotion blog—
www.hearmorefromGod.wordpress.com

LISTEN UP!
Lean in & Learn from the Lord™

Additional Thoughts on Praying for Character

More from Adventure Experience Press

Adventure Devos: The first devotional written exclusively for men with a heart for Risk and Danger

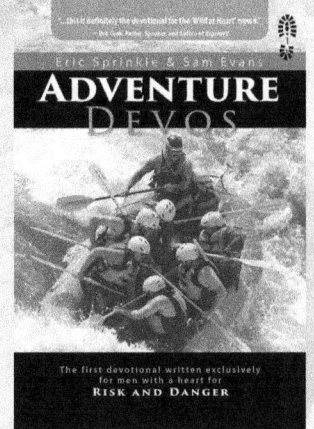

Adventure Devos: Women's Edition: An exciting devotional written exclusively for women with a Heart for Risk and Adventure

Adventure Devos: Youth Edition: Summer Camp never has to end when your devotional takes you adventuring all year long!

"Adventure Devos will challenge any man to be a better father or husband in no time, no doubt about it. Just read a few of the book's "Dares" and see for yourself how easily this devotional will get anyone into applying God's Word.
Megan "Katniss" Autrey, Colorado Certified Whitewater Guide Instructor, Wife and Mother

Additional Thoughts on Praying for Character

40DayPrayerGuides.com

Looking for another 40-Day Prayer Journey? Want to share and inspire others with stories from your last one? Welcome to the 40 Day Prayer Guide Series!

Be the first to download and check samples of the latest Guides, always weeks before they're listed for sale!

- Download free samples to share with friends
- Have a look at what's coming next in the 40-Day Prayer Guides series
- Share thoughts, ideas, and praises from your own 40-day journeys!

"This is a powerful book and is very much needed."

"I know several in my church right now who I plan to give copies to—real prayer warriors who would love this tool!"
(Early Reader Feedback)

Come have a look, sign up for the Newsletter and be more inspired in your prayer life today!

Additional Thoughts on Praying for Character

www.ingramcontent.com/pod-product-compliance
Lightning Source LLC
Chambersburg PA
CBHW071853070526
44583CB00016B/1675